ENDORSEMENTS

I was ten years old when I first time I met a black man. I sat mesmerized by this articulate, captivating and out-of-this-world preacher. Nicholas Bengu of South Africa defined for me what "blackness" was: powerful, alive, believable and charming. Later I learned some disparaged blacks, something I found incongruous and confusing.

This man who early defined for me the African character was the same who led my friend and colleague Ebe to spiritual faith.

Ebenezer Sikakane's story is a narration of faith and troubling conflict. His life overlays the struggle of the Christian community in Africa as it wrestled with religiously supported racism we better know as apartheid.

This powerful rendition of his calling and career help us see the progression and interplaying of biblical faith and justice, as it seeks life and substance in a world struggling with demons of injustice.

I have witnessed the wisdom and courage of this man who in life and calling, manifests a profound faith of his Lord in both his teaching and leading.

This extraordinary book will remind you that while the grinding out of Christian life is never easy it is the only way.

—BRIAN STILLER

Ebenezer Sikakane portrays apartheid from an insider's point of view—that of the main object of the intended subjugation. But he refused to be subdued. Through his pursuit of education, his keen Christian faith, and his willingness to take risks, he persevered and won.

Among the many leaders of African Enterprise I have known, Ebe stands out among the rising black leadership. He excelled as a Zulu-English interpreter, being chosen for that role for Billy Graham when he came to South Africa.

His story is finally told here, lest such a reign of terror be repeated among new generations, and to see the power of the Gospel to set men free.

—REV. J. WILLIAM LAMB

WRESTLING WITH
APARTHEID

Corinna;

Thanks for your tirelessness
for the work of the gospel
"Wait upon God." Isa 40:31
Ebe
3/10/10

Ebenezer M. Sikakane

WRESTLING WITH APARTHEID

ISBN-13: 978-1-77069-009-7

Printed by Word Alive Press
131 Cordite Road, Winnipeg, MB R3W 1S1
www.wordalivepress.ca

WORD ALIVE PRESS
Just Write!

Dedicated to my late wife
of 55 years,
EMILY.

Library and Archives Canada Cataloguing in Publication

Sikakane, Ebenezer M.
    Wrestling with apartheid : an autobiography / Ebenezer M. Sikakane.

Includes bibliographical references.
ISBN 978-1-77069-009-7

    1. Sikakane, Ebenezer M. 2. Sikakane, Ebenezer M--Family.
3. Evangelists--
Canada--Biography. 4. Evangelists--South Africa--Biography.
5. Missionaries--
South Africa--Biography. 6. Apartheid--South Africa. I. Title.

BV3785.S49A3 2010   269'.2092   C2010-903422-8

INTRODUCTION

Apartheid needs no introduction. People all over the world have heard about the wicked systematic suffering experienced by blacks in South Africa until the oppressive white government was voted out of office in 1994. Ebenezer Sikakane was born and bred in South Africa, where he saw and experienced apartheid firsthand. In fact, the author is writing this in Canada where he and his wife, Emily, now live with their five grown children and nine grandchildren, who were all born in Canada. Before deciding to immigrate, he had learned from reliable sources that the white government was going take him in for interrogation—a terrifying ordeal for a socially active black. So he fled the country with his family.

Settlers of Dutch descent first came to South Africa in 1652. They became known as Afrikaners, or Boers (Dutch for "farmer"), and they spoke Afrikaans, a corruption of the Netherlands' language. They were members of the Dutch Reformed

Church, and Calvinist in doctrine. They were followed by those of English descent in 1820, who were also Protestant (Anglican, Presbyterian, and Methodist, among others). The history of the land reflects a constant struggle between three groups: English settlers, Dutch settlers, and the black tribal groups. They fought the Boer War (1899-1902), which resulted in the forming of the Union of South Africa, which became part of the British Empire. But relationships continued to be strained between the English and Afrikaners.

Apartheid was a system of legislated racism perpetuated by Afrikaners. It was aimed at keeping blacks from having any say in the political governing of their own country. Laws discriminating against blacks were enacted and enforced with fierce brutality. Legislation after legislation was passed, ensuring that there was absolutely no loophole left unsealed by law. The Job Reservation Act protected all the jobs that were reserved for whites. The Bantu Education Act was designed to cripple blacks' education by giving them inferior education. The Group Areas Act assigned each racial group places where they could live and operate their businesses. Blacks lived in rural areas outside cities. There were "WHITES ONLY" signs everywhere in cities indicating where blacks were not welcome—from theatres to toilets. Public counters were segregated in banks and post offices. The government even had a dedicated police force to enforce these laws with barbarous brutality. These police were second to none in the world. There was a radio program showcasing the courage of the police, which aired this tagline: *They protect the people of South Africa.*" It should have been: *"They protect the **white** people of South Africa."*

The people of South Africa were neatly divided into four categories by the Population Registration Act: Whites, Asians, Coloureds, and Bantu, in that descending order of preference. "Whites" were the Dutch Afrikaners and the English, representing 15.5% of the total population. "Coloureds" were those who were neither white nor black, but of mixed race: 8.8% of the population. "Asians" was the term denoting settlers who had come from India: 2.7%. The "Bantu" were the blacks, an overwhelming majority of 70.4%.[1] Whites were on top in everything, and blacks right at the bottom. Whites were the highest paid. Coloureds were next, and then the Asians. Blacks were at the bottom of the pile. Blacks were so deeply trapped at the bottom of the pile that whereas the other "non-whites" could live and trade on the fringes of the cities, blacks couldn't. Whereas other non-whites could apply for passports, blacks were required to pay a deposit of four hundred rands so that, upon return, they would surrender the passport and get their money back. The reason for this that the authorities could keep track of where and why they were coming and going from the country.

Bantustans

Bantustans were district enclaves in South Africa, created by the apartheid regime, where blacks were supposed to govern

---

[1] These percentages are based on the total population of South Africa in 1981, which was 28,393,000.

themselves along their own tribal lines. Bantustans were designed as "homelands" for black people. They began in earnest around 1948 when the Afrikaners, led by Dr. D.F. Malan, won the elections—the same year in which seventeen-year-old Ebenezer ("Ebe") became a Christian. It was not until Dr. Hendrik Verwoerd became the prime minister that Bantustans truly took shape. He was really the architect of the government's Separate Development policy. Verwoerd, a bright man, fine-tuned the policy of apartheid like no other prime minister before him. He deceptively tried to create the impression that once his evil system was completed, the ten or so resulting black states would be totally autonomous and would all live together harmoniously as "equals" in their parallel states. All this was imposed on blacks without any consultation. And most blacks did not want it. Verwoerd later died a painful death when he was stabbed with a knife as he was rising to address Parliament in Cape Town in 1966.

The law selected the best land and declared it "white"— leaving the worst land to be given to each tribe. The government drew borders that zigzagged around all the best land. They found tribal heads for these homelands, whom they called "Chief Ministers." Each of these homelands would have all the facilities they needed to make them self-governing and self-sufficient. The townships outside white cities would be built along tribal lines as well. A good model for what took place is what happened in Soweto ("SOuth WEstern TOwnships"), a regional group of these townships. Some of the Sowetan townships had tribal names, but the older ones kept their English and Afrikaans names, like White City, Meadowlands, and Dobsonville. These holdouts, who were brain-washed by the government, would ultimately change their minds and accept the plan to adopt tribal names. The newly appointed Chief Ministers visited these new "urban dwellers" in their townships so that the Sowetans could keep in touch with their rural roots, where they really belonged.

Some of the Chief Ministers accepted self-government and were declared autonomous. Others, like the chief of amaZulu, who was supposedly to become the Chief Minister, refused to take amaZulu to a quasi-independence. That was the reason he ran against Chief Nelson Mandela for presidency of the first democratic South Africa. Those who fell for the offer made by the white regime discovered that no country in the world was prepared to recognize their "homelands," despite the efforts of the regime to assure them of the genuineness of their independence.

One of these chiefs was a born again Christian man, Chief Mangophe. He had a remarkable conversion in East London, in the former Cape Province of South Africa. He was attending the Nicholas Bhengu's Annual Convention, held from Boxing Day through New Year's Day. Ebenezer's wife Emily was there as well, and she described Mangophe's conversion as spectacular. He had come to the convention all the way from the former Northern Transvaal Province. Mangophe, who was a respected chief in his homeland, called Bophuthatswana, went public with his conversion. The story of his conversion reverberated throughout the whole of South Africa because this popular convention was attended by people from each of the four former provinces: Cape Province, Natal, Orange Free State, and Transvaal.

Bantu Affairs Minister

The white government apparently believed that they had to do anything they could to persuade black people to accept Separate Development, or Parallel Development. They went to great lengths and extremes canvassing for support. Any cabinet minister who was assigned the portfolio of Bantu Affairs had a portfolio that was envied by all. He was at the heart of the most important matter in South Africa. He really became a "government" in and of himself. Dr. Herzog, who was the Minister of Health, was reported as having said that he hardly slept at night thinking about the danger posed by blacks. He said he closed one eye and the other was opened, watching the activities of this "black danger," or *swart gevaar*. If he could say that, imagine what the minister in charge of the *swart gevaar* would have said?

One example will suffice. There were about six thousand independent churches in South Africa. They were all led by blacks, most of whom had never been to a Bible college. Some could barely read the Bible. They almost despised black people who went to churches led by white ministers or missionaries. Some of these independent churches were very small. There were often just a couple of families, and they would simply meet under a tree if the weather was good—and it is often good in South Africa, the land of sunshine. Some of the churches, however, were huge. They are still huge, like the

Zion Christian Church (ZCC), founded in 1910 in the former Transvaal Province. The president of South Africa did not only give audience to its leader, Lekganyana, but actually visited Lekganyana's "palace" in person during his Easter services.

It was alleged that Lekganyana's followers rented practically all the Putco (Public Utilities Transportation Company, which transported blacks throughout Johannesburg and the black townships) buses to move his church members from Johannesburg, and other cities, to Pietersburg, where his headquarters were situated. Imagine the president appearing before those crowds, putting his seal of approval to what they were doing and assuring them of his blessing. This served as excellent public relations for the Head of State, who was coming to promote his Bantustan policy. Every official was, in fact, engaged in this kind of policy promotion—giving the people a very hollow hope of a glorious future in their homelands. They were the good guys, and the black politicians and freedom fighters (terrorists) were the bad guys, deceived by communists. A similar message was given to some foreign tourists coming from abroad as guests of the regime. The president's message to Lekganyana and his thousands of followers was that they were the model of the government policy.

Some of the things blacks were not allowed or do were as follows. They could not vote, because they were not citizens of their own country. They could not join the army, because they had no country to defend. No employment statistics were available for them, because they were not included—even in the unemployment statistics. They paid no income tax, but they did pay what was called "head tax"—and it cost every man a whole two pounds, ten shillings sterling, which was a heavy burden. They had no retirement, no pensions, no trade unions, no paid maternity leave for mothers. They carried a thick passbook, which they had to produce upon demand by a police officer or any government official. Failure to do so was a punishable offence.

TABLE OF CONTENTS

I

PLACE OF BIRTH AND EDUCATION

Ebe and Emily were born and brought up in South Africa. Ebe was born on January 1, 1931, in a small rural area outside a town called Estcourt—in the land of apartheid. He was the last of eight children—four boys and four girls—born to Daniel and Esther Sikakane. His parents never went to school. His dad attended an informal night school in Kimberley, where he was a security watchman in a diamond mine. They walked days on end to get to Kimberley from the province of Natal. He was left-handed, and it was believed that such people were not supposed to attempt to write. But he did learn to read the Bible and became a lay preacher in a small rural Baptist church. Emily was born near a town called Newcastle in what was then Northern Natal. Her parents had minimum education as well. They could both read and write isiZulu. Her dad was a lay preacher in the Methodist Church. He worked in Johannesburg and managed to buy and own land before the apartheid regime put a stop to blacks buying land and obtaining valid title deeds. His group formed a syndicate group of landowners. Her parents, Eliam and Elizabeth Sibisi, had three girls and two boys. Emily was the middle child.

Ebenezer's Village

Ebenezer was born in a rural area assigned to his tribe by the white government.

It was a very isolated area with a couple of trading stores many miles away and far apart. A trip to either of these stores took more than half a day. This meant that people had to depend almost entirely on the produce from their own field. Homes were widely separated. Nobody had "neighbours," at least not in the modern sense. There had to be a lot of land between families, because the families were big. When each son got married and started a family of his own, they were added to his parents' home. He could expand as he was able. This resulted in many large homes in the district. In spite of this, there was good understanding and relationships between them. Each district formed communities that were loyal to each other. They formed a tribe under one chief and did a lot of things together. There would be one area where people sent their cows, goats, and sheep for grazing. There would be another area reserved for them to grow their food produce.

When Ebe was still a young man, the government decided that the district where he was growing up was going to be turned into a game reserve. Wild animals were to roam freely in the area, and everyone had to move away from it. The head men and their chief tried in vain to get the government to assign them an alternative area where they could settle as a tribe. They were told that their land was going to be ruined by soil erosion. Human beings moved out and animals moved in. Indeed, many years afterwards, when Ebe was driven by a nephew to the site where he was born and bred, he found that ostriches and other wild animals had taken possession of their large, unoccupied home.

The family was scattered all over the eastern region that is now called KwaZulu-Natal Province. His eldest brother ventured deep into what was then known as the heart of Zululand. They were hoping to find the same kind of life they'd enjoyed before, this time between the towns of Estcourt and Weenen, where they could hopefully live with little interference from whites. It was not to be! The second brother settled in a mission station called Ekuphumuleni, meaning "at rest," outside a town called Empangeni. He certainly found rest there—rest for his soul, because before long he and his wife were soundly converted. (Their firstborn, who later lived with Ebe and Emily, became a Christian while living with them.) The third brother also moved elsewhere in Zululand, but soon passed away at the Springfield T.B. (tuberculosis) hospital in Durban. Just before he died, he had put his faith in Christ as Ebe visited him there. He asked his youngest brother to get into the hospital shower and baptize him, but the young Christian, Ebe, didn't dare do such a thing. He thought that it was something only an ordained minister should do. So he could only pray with him.

WRESTLING WITH APARTHEID

Primary Schooling (1939)

One of the major problems that faced young blacks in South Africa was education. Young people growing up in rural areas did not even know they were being deprived of something so important. White children had the luxury of attending school. Secondly, education was possible for only the small percentage of people who had opportunities to enter schools—and these were mainly young people living near cities and small towns. It was free and compulsory for well-to-do whites. But black people had no money to pay for the education of their children. Thirdly, there was no incentive to get an education, since there were no attractive jobs for blacks. It should be added, however, that those who did get opportunities, and embraced them, get everything out of them that they could. Some of the early missionaries did an excellent job of educating blacks within their mission stations, and probably beyond.

The first school Ebe attended was in a small one-room church building, built of wattle and daub, which was approximately six kilometres away from home. A lady teacher, who was probably unqualified, was the sole teacher in the school. The next school he went to was in a similar Roman Catholic church building. There was one lady teacher there as well. The schools progressively improved until he entered a higher primary school in Weenen, and then began high school in Wasbank in 1947. This was a couple of hours away by two trains, travelling from Weenen to Wasbank. Going to school by train! Wow! What a treat! Emily's early schooling situation was similar, except that it was slightly better than Ebe's. She started high school in a good Roman Catholic private school, taught by excellent nuns. She and a few other girls were somewhat discriminated against because they were Protestants.

Before going to Wasbank, Ebe was thinking about furthering his education. Where would he go? How could he get there? Where would he find money to pay for a high school education? But by this time, his dad was retired, somewhat early, without pension. His mother was the one who was really keen to get her son educated. Any bit of craft work she could make and sell, though, wouldn't get her nearly close enough to pay for her eighth baby. She had high hopes for him, wanting him to be so educated that he could fly on *flamashini* (flying machines). But it was just a pipe dream, people thought as they laughed. She lived to see him fly for the first time to preach at Mseleni Mission with the principal of Union Bible Institute. (Incidentally, Ebe has flown more than seven hundred times— he kept a record of his flights).

Mike, a friend of Ebe's whom he had met in higher primary school in Weenen, was to go to school in Wasbank. He was to stay with Cleopas, a school teacher from Ebe's district. There was no time to ask Cleopas if Ebe could come, too. Ebe simply boarded the train with Mike to Wasbank without any prior arrangements made with Cleopas. They would simply get off the train together!

"Where are you going, Ebenezer?" Cleopas asked when both boys got off the train together.

With a broad smile, Ebe said, "I am coming to school here with Mike."

Ebe naively expected him to say, "Wonderful"! Instead, he was dumb-founded. There was no prearranged accommodation. Ebe was completely oblivious to the seriousness of what he had done to Cleopas. The decision had been quickly made by Mike and Ebe without even the knowledge of their parents. The parents had been under the impression that Cleopas knew about Ebe's coming. Ebe ended up staying with the principal after a month, a Mr. S.S. Nyandeni. Ebe thought he had it made there—sleeping on benches in a classroom next door to the principal's room. He did all the chores for him, learning to clean up, sweep the floor, and prepare breakfast. He did well in school.

College Education

From high school, Ebe took a shortcut to a teacher training college without matriculation. So did Emily. This shortcut was created for black people only. The feeling of the apartheid government was that black people did not need higher education like whites did. Ebe heard about St. Chad's College, near a town called Ladysmith, that trained teachers. It was an Anglican college, which did admit students from other denominations. He applied and was accepted. His dad was going to sell a cow to put him through teacher training college, but about a week and a half before college reopened, he received a letter from St. Chad's College withdrawing his acceptance! They had to admit Anglicans who had applied late.

In a big quandary, Ebe took a train to Wasbank, where Mr. S.S. Nyandeni was principal of the high school which Ebe had attended. He hoped Nyandeni would be able to help him, for he had heard about a new teacher training college near Vryheid, but had no details whatsoever. Upon some inquiry, Ebe found that a classmate in his school, named Fortesque, had received forms from this new college but had decided on a different one. Ebe was able to get Fortesque's forms and fill them out with Mr. Nyandeni's help. After a while, however, they came to a strange question which asked, "Are you a Christian?" The answer was "Yes." The next question was, "When did you become a Christian?" After puzzling this one out, it was suggested that he write, "By birth."

The name of the new college was the Evangelical Teacher Training College (ETTC). A phone call revealed that spaces were still available. ETTC was established by missionaries working in South Africa and was opening its doors for the first time in 1948. It was here that Ebe talked to whites for the first time. He had seen them from a distance, but now he met with them face to face. The headmaster, Nolan Balman, a graduate of Wheaton College, in the United States, and who was with The Evangelical Alliance Mission (TEAM), met the new student at the door, and shook his hand and asked, "Are you Mr. Sikakane"? This blew Ebe away. He was the first white man to shake hands with him, and the first person to address him as "Mr." This served as an introduction to the Christian atmosphere that permeated the entire college. Students were immersed in it. The principal of ETTC, Mr. Herbert Barrett, was a Canadian from Three Hills, Alberta who served with South Africa General Mission (SAGM), which later became the African Evangelical Fellowship (AEF). It is now known as

SIM International (Serving In Mission). Several other teachers were missionaries from the United States, Canada, the United Kingdom, and Sweden. They were equally courteous and passionate about sharing the Gospel with students. They sang choruses, read the Bible, and prayed before each class. There were also devotionals for the whole student body every morning. Christian speakers were invited to speak to the students all the time. Some of the teachers who made an impression on Ebe were African teachers who were part and parcel of this Christian Institution.

During the second half of Ebe's first year, the college invited a black evangelist, Nicholas Bhengu, to speak. Bhengu was probably the greatest evangelist that South Africa had ever seen. He had just returned from a preaching tour of the United States. He came and preached daily in chapel from just one verse of the Bible—John 3:16. And for ten days, it was always about John 3:16!

The illustrations he used in his messages were very effective. One of them was the story about a rich white man who lived during the days when the use of a motor car was rare. This farmer's daughter was about to get married. He and his wife took her shopping. Before returning home, he asked the daughter to sit on their horse-drawn carriage while they went to buy her a special wedding present. It was to be a surprise. While waiting there, the horses became frightened and wildly took off with the helpless girl, who didn't know what to do— she simply screamed her heart out. The louder she screamed, the faster the horses ran! One young man noticed what was happening. As the horses approached him, he made a daring attempt to save her. He courageously jumped onto the carriage and barely stopped the horses. In the process, the young man seriously hurt his back, ending up in a wheelchair. This superb storyteller painted a vivid description of the characters, often with great humour.

Her parents proceeded with preparations for her wedding. They took her to the hospital to visit the young man who had saved her life. She proposed the postponement of the wedding until she saw how he was doing. She finally decided she was going to marry the man who had saved her life, despite her parents' objections and all the other offers of lifetime support the disabled young man had received. She made an irreversible decision to spend the rest of her life with the man who gave himself for her. Nicholas marshalled his evangelistic skill in convincing each student to make the obvious decision for Christ, to follow Him who had done much more than the wheelchair man. The students who had been on the floor with laughter were now on their knees before the cross of Calvary.

According to Ebe, "On the evening of August 28, the preacher seemed to direct his message to me and to no other student. I brought up all sorts of excuses in my heart, and the preacher answered each one as though he had a list of them in front of him on the pulpit. When I exhausted my excuses, the preacher concluded his message. Under the crushing conviction, I surrendered my life to Jesus Christ. A dramatic transformation took place in my life. I had the soundest sleep of my life that night. The morning brought a brand new creation around me, so it seemed. I then began to pray, hiding under the staircase, that the Lord would take me away before the end of the year. I knew I could not face my Estcourt friends who were awaiting me. I had sung in a quartet with them. I knew the pressure I would face. It was nothing but lustful mischief that had motivated us to form that quartet: we wanted to get all the beautiful girls in town. That prayer was obviously not answered the way I expected it to be. My faith did survive in some amazing ways."

In his final year, Ebe met a young petite first year beauty from Newcastle, who was introduced to him by a friend. He describes Emily's beauty as being absolutely stunning. He was supposed to start dating her. He did before someone else beat him to it. But one did not date in South Africa. ETTC was particularly strict on this point, being an evangelical institution. Boys did, nevertheless, date creatively. Guys were not allowed to talk to girls, but they found ways of passing notes back and forth. Later in the year, Emily gave her life to Christ when two TEAM missionaries on their way to Mosvold Hospital stopped by, and Dr. Taylor spoke in chapel on the subject of the rich young ruler (Luke 18). It was such a joy for Ebe to see her respond to the Gospel, as he had done.

The rules were so strict that student letters sent and received even from their parents and friends were read by the matron before being handed to students or sealed by the matron and mailed out. But the kids' internal "mail delivery system" was hard to track down. Even though the dining room was wisely segregated with girls occupying tables on the east and guys on the west, with the faculty table forming a buffer in the centre of the dining room, communication went on! After Ebe graduated, he wrote to Herbert Barrett, the principal, making his confession and assuring him that they were planning to get married. In his response, Mr. Barrett quoted John's epistle, "I was overjoyed to find some of my children walking in the truth" (2 John 4).

There was a young missionary teacher, a nurse by profession, who came to ETTC the same year as Emily. She taught Physiology and Hygiene to both Ebe's graduating class and Emily's freshman class. She was Betty Flory from Doylestown, Pennsylvania. She was friendly, and came to know a number of the students. She asked Ebe to assist her when male students came to the dispensary that she was responsible for. She asked Emily to assist when the girls had their turn in the dispensary. She had obviously noticed them both on the few occasions when guys and girls could sit together in an evening social programme when the whole staff attended. Ebe always sat next to Emily. She told Ebe without asking him that he was interested in her. Ebe "fessed up." She also liked Emily very much, which was why she chose Emily to assist her. She prayed with each one and discipled them separately before opening the dispensary. At one point, she took Ebe to a white dentist in Vryheid for a filling. The dentist told her "NO," and very emphatically. You do not fill black peoples teeth, she was told. You pull them out. She pleaded without success, and became a bit upset. She was called onto the carpet by the college after the dentist warned the college officials about her!

Betty got married to another American missionary who was a widower, Melvin Swanson. The couple ended up adopting Ebe and Emily. To this day, at age 88 and 86, living in a retirement home, she and her husband still regard Sikakanes as their eldest kids. When the Sikakanes moved to Canada, the couple took one of their two daughters, Primrose, and got her into Pinebrook College in Pennsylvaia. Their own children helped to raise funds for the Sikakane family to move to North America when they fled South Africa in 1978.

There were two good choirs at ETTC. Ebe sang in Choir A, which was led by a very bright young musician, Mr. Ngwenya. Emily joined Choir B with members of her freshman class. In addition to this, four guys including Ebe formed a quartet. It turned out to be a good public relations quartet for the school. They called themselves *Sea Birds*. The first time they sang in an evening social, Mrs. Barrett was so moved that she sent for her husband to come and hear them. So they gave a repeat performance of that great Negro Spiritual, "Ezekiel Saw de Wheel." The school then organized a couple of trips for the quartet to tour mission churches in KwaZulu-Natal. They toured around, singing and sharing their testimonies.

Ebe spent his long winter breaks—not summer breaks, as in North America—finding jobs to earn enough money to return to college. The best job he got was at a petrol (gas) station in Estcourt. One day, the white owner pointed him out to his wife. He wondered what was happening. Ebe ended up working in her kitchen because he misled her by saying that he had no money to return to school. She wanted him to be her permanent kitchen boy. The couple took him to Durban to see the ocean for the first time. They seemed surprised that Ebe wanted to go to school so badly, because their white kids were not so enthusiastic about school. When the time came for him to return to college, he went to Mrs. Felgate and said, "Missus,

I have found enough money to return to college." She was terribly disappointed but could not stop him. As Ebe continued to grow in his faith, he was later so convicted that he wrote a letter of full confession to her, but she did not respond. There were many other areas in Ebe's life that called for restitution, and he never hesitated to provide it.

The one great experience Ebe had at ETTC was that of graduation. He had never seen one before. He did not know what it was all about. They talked a lot about it as the day was approaching. To his amazement, he was chosen to be the valedictorian, because he had done well academically. They had an excellent English teacher at ETTC, Miss Joan Scutt, a lady from England who was a missionary in Swaziland. She was very strict. She was the first teacher from England to teach them English. In their freshman class, an energetic Miss Rose Gertiser-Hicks was the English teacher and secretary of ETTC. Joan took over from her. Joan soon got the reputation for wanting "everything to be grammatically correct." When the first graduation came around, Joan had gone back to Swaziland where she was a missionary. She was leaving a great legacy behind. There were about five students whom she thought were getting a good grasp of English grammar, and they included Ebe.

As expected, when he returned to Estcourt after his encounter with Christ, he gave his testimony, telling the group that he could no longer be a part of the quartet. They brushed it aside and tried to convince him that it was just a passing feeling. They approached him again and again, but they always met the same response. Without him knowing, they connived together and came up with something they were sure he would not turn down. Two guys arranged for a car to take the group to a party in the Drakensburg Mountains area. On their way out, they stopped for Ebe, called him out to the car, and showed him four pretty girls—"doves," as they called them. "The fourth one is yours, bro," said the organizer to me. When he turned that one down, humiliating the "dove" chosen for him, they realized he wasn't going to change his mind. That was the last time they bothered with Ebe.

II
TEACHING CAREER
(1950-1956)

The Norwegian Mission Union (NMU) director, a Swedish missionary, approached the ETTC principal and asked him to recommend a graduate for one of his schools, of which he was the "Grantee," or manager (on behalf of the government). Ebe was selected, and he soon left home by train to start teaching in the district of Stanger just northeast of Durban, at the Ekuthandaneni School. Before long, Ebe shared the Gospel with students, and the school was in a state of revival. Neighbouring schools began to notice what was happening at Ekuthandaneni. He found himself preaching in other schools as well. He had a good team of born again teachers who were very committed to Christ and to the proclamation of the Gospel. Two lady teachers were graduates of ETTC. They were older than Ebe and they were very spiritually mature. In fact, there was a large group of mature young people in the Norwegian Mission Union. There were a dozen other churches that enjoyed good fellowship with NMU. One could easily have mistook them for Pentecostals. They believed and preached holiness. Ebe and Emily owe their spiritual growth to this group. They ranged from teachers to maids. In fact, one of these maids, Diana Gumede, who worked for rich family, the Balcombs, who lived in Kearsney near Stanger, supported Ebe when he attended the Union Bible Institute.

Swapping Schools

The next thing Ebe knew, Emily was appointed to another one of the mission's schools, called Glendale Primary School. When the Grantee needed a principal at Glendale, he promoted Ebe. But to send him to Glendale, he had to transfer Emily to Ekuthandaneni. They could not let a "dating" couple work together in the same church school, because that was not a good testimony. He could not get into her room. She could never get into his. Even going to a city together was "frowned upon." They had to walk in the light and be blameless before the watching world. They were happy to swap schools.

The continuing revival led them to convene a youth camp at their school in order to strengthen young people in their faith. Neighbouring schools were invited. A good number from the neighbouring schools had come on board. They spent a weekend of Bible teaching at the mission station. One evening, Ebe was interpreting for a Norwegian missionary who had just come to South Africa who was a dynamic speaker despite his weak English. That night, he spoke on the call of Samuel, *"Speak Lord, for your servant is listening"* (1 Samuel

3:9, NIV). Ebe knew that the Lord was calling him out of teaching into some other ministry. He was very convicted, even though he was interpreting. He walked forward to be prayed for together with the young people who crowded the altar. After that, he continued working as though nothing had happened. It was not until the Word of the Lord came to him a second time, that he did something about it! This time the word came from Acts 26:19: *"I was not disobedient to the vision from heaven"* (NIV). On this occasion, another missionary from Sweden was preaching at an Easter convention that had brought together all Norwegian congregations plus other friendly neighbouring local churches with which they had fellowship. After that, Ebe was readying himself for going to Bible School.

What Led to Promotion to Principalship

School inspectors never warned that they would be coming to inspect the school. They simply showed up. Inspector Greene Buthelezi did just that while the classes were concluding morning devotions. Unfortunately, the principal was away. He had not told any of the teachers when he was going to arrive back at the school. The unwritten law was that, in the principal's absence, Ebe would act as principal. So Ebe provided the inspector with all the information he needed: the attendance of teachers and the number of pupils in their classes, daily class attendance registers, the logbook, and the school meals records. Ebe kept running back and forth between the office where the inspector was and the classrooms where the teachers and pupils were.

This incredible morning resulted in something good for Ebe. As usual, the inspector would pay a courtesy call to the Grantee before leaving the school. So, in a meeting with the Grantee, Reverend N.P. Hagemann, the absence of the principal and Ebe's performance as his Substitute was discussed.. A few days after the departure of the inspector, the Grantee indicated that Ebe had done a good job of managing the school in the principal's absence. The two men agreed that Ebe would be in a position of being principal in one of the schools under the Grantee's jurisdiction. It was those two leaders who identified some potential that ended up getting Ebe to that job.

III
THE GREAT EVENT

Emily's dad was not happy that his daughter wanted to marry someone who seemed to be an unknown nonentity to him, whereas there were local boys whose families he respected and who were in his "class" and with whom he had formed a respectable syndicate. But these two held their engagement party in Stanger. Shortly afterwards, on June 2, 1954, Emily placed Ebe "in her file"—and he has been there ever since! It was not a big earth-shattering affair, but rather a very modest one, because they were not sure that her dad was going to give her away in marriage. He did! By then, Ebe had returned to Ekuthandaneni as principal of that combined primary school. It was only then that they taught together for two years.

Their first child was born at the prestigious McCord Hospital in Durban. Emily brought back an incredible, bouncing baby boy, Ebenson. Little Ebenson was literally displayed on their dining room table, when all of the school's staff members came to meet him. He is now a school teacher in Toronto, Ontario. He was followed by an equally bouncing baby girl, Rosemary, born at the same hospital. She is now a nurse manager at the University of Minnesota. Their third sister, Primrose, came and now works for a major insurance company in downtown Toronto. Finally, our family doctor just about floored us when he announced that Emily was carrying twins! Our twin boys are both in computers—Crown is in Toronto and Wiseman is in Minnesota, where he manages a computer department.

The entire family, as well as Ebe's father-in-law, soon learned that what God has joined together cannot be separated. Emily was never deterred. She showed great determination to go through with the wedding. A few years after the marriage, her dad visited the family's home in Pietermaritzburg, Natal. From that day and every subsequent visit he made to Ebe and Emily's home, he was very apologetic for nearly spoiling such a good marriage for his daughter. He assured them that their home was beyond comparison to those of his friends back in Newcastle. Ebe had never heard an umZulu father apologize so profusely to his children.

IV
MINISTRY TRAINING AND TEACHING (1956-1969)

E be and Emily considered their call into the ministry very carefully. Emily had initially been unsure about the wisdom of giving up his principalship and going to Union Bible Institute. They knew of no Zulu pastor of the evangelical church who had high education. Ebe had just completed the National Senior Certificate, which was about the equivalent of matriculation (Emily was to do that later). Ebe got an increment by being promoted to principalship, and a further increment after completing N.S.C. He was going to forfeit all this by going to Bible School. It was a serious decision to make. Once Emily was convinced that this was the way the Lord was leading them, she stood by it in spite of all the trying times they faced from the first year. She was actually carrying the thicker end of the stick, supporting herself and the baby, because she was teaching. Towards the completion of Ebe's first year, she discovered that they had their second child on the way. So she had to stop teaching. Ebe quickly notified the school that he was going to have to go back and teach for a year. When he told Emily of his decision, she firmly advised him to withdraw that notice. She assured him that God, who is able to supply the needs of widows, would supply the needs of the family. And He did.

The years Ebe spent at the Union Bible Institute, studying the Word of God, were unequalled. His eyes were opened to the truths of Scripture in ways that he could never have anticipated. The Swedish principal, Reverend Bernard Johanson, who had studied at Moody Bible Institute, was an incredible exponent of Scripture, teacher of the Word, and preacher of the Gospel. The class simply ate up everything he taught them. Johanson was a prolific author of books in isiZulu. He spoke isiZulu fluently, having learned it from both his dad and from amaZulu, among whom he grew up. He wrote many Bible commentaries, most of which became school textbooks. There were other white missionaries who taught at UBI (Union Bible Institute), on loan from missions that sent students there. Though Ebe, who was the only black teacher at that point, was paid by UBI, the others were paid by their missions.

The very first year Ebe was enrolled, he was given the responsibility of training and directing the school's male voice choir. It was a terrific choir. They sang acappella.

Several years later, a ladies Bible School joined U.B.I from Mhlotsheni, Swaziland. After that happened, he found himself leading a mixed voice choir. The second year, he started proofreading all the books the principal wrote as they were printed at the Mission Press in Durban. The author taught him how to do that job professionally. This was the beginning of what Ebe did after he joined the teaching staff.

Bernard Johanson had his eyes on Ebe as his possible successor for principalship upon his retirement. He alluded to this several times. He was being "groomed." Ebe also managed the sale of books when students took books home with them to sell during vacation. He checked the book orders and cash when the students returned, giving them their commission. He wrote Sunday school materials that were published monthly in a magazine called UBAQA (Light of the World). It was discovered that lots of untrained pastors used these notes to preach from in their Sunday services.

Ebe was taught driving and earned a heavy-duty license so that he could drive the truck to pick up building material and other supplies from the city during the week. On weekends, the truck became a bus, with Ebe as the driver. Benches were fitted in the back with a canopy overhead to keep out sun and rain. By this means, UBI students were dropped off at churches where they taught Sunday Schools, while other students went on with Ebe to the nearest township. There, they set up a sound system and held an evangelistic meeting. Students would give testimonies, while another would preach a message. Converts would be counselled. Then the truck would return, picking up all the students, and return in time for lunch. In the early afternoon, similar meetings were held in the black townships around the city of Pietermaritzburg. In this way, the students gained practical experience to supplement their studies.

Ebe learned to record, copy, and file isiZulu messages preached by the principal in his morning devotions, and made copies for sale. Eventually, Ebe was appointed the registrar. He was encouraged also to start writing books in his mother tongue, and ended up with ten isiZulu booklets. He donated his manuscripts to the school and received no royalties for them. He interpreted a number of other books into his language.

Talk about a heavy job description! That was never in anyone's vocabulary. No one spoke about salary. They earned twelve pounds, ten shillings a month. He and Emily, with their five children, were assisted by the honoraria they got when he went out and spoke at youth camps and Bible weeks, evangelistic meetings during vacation weeks. Eventually, he came to be booked well ahead of these weeks. These invitations supplemented their salary and were very helpful.

Bernard Johanson, a Visionary

This was evident in his ministry. Ebe thought, in hindsight, that it was clear from the relationship he had with Bernard Johanson that the man saw something in him he never knew he had. Bernard took his time mentoring him and expressing in no uncertain terms that his was hope was that Ebe would take over as principal when he retired. All the duties that Bernard handed to Ebe were obviously meant to prepare him for the future ministry. He thought it was necessary that the responsibility was given to an African instead of to another missionary struggling with culture and language. Some missionaries did not see eye to eye with Bernard's plan, as some of them aspired to succeed Bernard. Also, some of them wouldn't want to serve under a black principal in apartheid South Africa.

Emily's Perspective

Emily said, "We faced problems from time to time as our family grew. These were mostly health problems. I remember teaching at Burton Farm Primary School when my husband was at Union Bible Institute. I was home alone with the children when my daughter became seriously ill and I didn't know what to do. I didn't know what she was suffering from. I did not have any money. There was no clinic anywhere nearby. We had no means of transport. I did everything I could to help her. In desperation, I carried the baby with me and took a long walk, not knowing where I was going. I continued with the most important I could do, and that was to pray for her. I occasionally glanced to see and feel if she was still breathing. In the evening, I heard hymn singing coming from a home in the neighbourhood. They were having a prayer meeting. I took the baby there and asked them to pray for her. I knew the lady who was the leader of the women who were gathered for prayer. They prayed for her. She made it through the night. The leader came again the next morning to see how the baby was doing. Finally, she improved.

"Something else happened when we were at Union Bible Institute. Rosemary seemed to have the flu while my husband was in class teaching. While I was waiting for him, a student we knew just came to see how we were doing. He saw that Rosemary was not well. He prayed and left. Then he turned around and knocked on the door again. He then handed me fifty cents and said, 'Buy her some oranges.' He didn't know that we did not have fifty cents in the house. My husband came home and he hired the school vehicle right away, and we were going to pay for it at the end of the month. We took the child to the clinic in Pietermaritzburg. Blacks paid very little at the clinic. So we paid forty cents admission and had ten cents change left over to buy oranges!

"After several such problems, not just health ones but financial ones as well, I decided to find a job. It was generally regarded as unspiritual for a minister's wife to work. You did that when you had stopped trusting God to provide for your needs. In fact, earlier I had turned down a teaching position right on the church property adjoining U.B.I. When I later looked for a teaching position, there were none available. We had agreed that I had to find some income, as the children were growing and we were no longer able to stretch the rand any further. I found a job at a laundry where I ironed men's shirts. I started work at 6:30 a.m. and finished at 6 p.m. It did not last too long because I found an opening in a school close to U.B.I. So I started teaching again."

That improved the family's cash flow a great deal.

MINISTRY TRAINING AND TEACHING

Emily, Ebe's Helpmate

Ebe would like to add his personal footnote to Emily's paragraph.

"When I packed my bags and left for U.B.I., Emily stayed home to teach and look after our firstborn. It was not long after I was getting deep into my schoolwork that she wrote and let me know that we had a second baby on the way. After thinking and praying about the whole situation, I came to the conclusion that there was no way Emily could manage without the income that she received as a teacher. I went to the late Reverend Abner Mndebele, who was the house master and a dynamic Bible teacher from Swaziland, and I explained the situation to him. I had to return home at the end of the term. He discussed it with the principal. I got two responses, one from Emily and the other from the school. They were basically saying the same thing. Emily had said, 'If the Lord is able to support widows, He will never fail to support me.' The Principal reminded me, 'The Lord is able to provide all your needs.'"

Ebe began to see things happening from that time on. Emily received unexpected registered letters with cash from friends. Ebe occasionally found envelopes on his desk with cash. White ladies from Chapel Street Baptist Church sent a large carton full of everything that the baby and his older brother would need and use for a long time.

Emily proved to be a real "helper," not just by cooking and doing laundry for her family, but by encouraging Ebe to press on with his studies then and in future years at the University of South Africa, the Fuller School of World Missions, and later at Trinity Evangelical Divinity School. On a number of occasion, he would decide to drop his studies because of his workload, but she was insistent.

One discouragement he got came from failing one of the three major courses that every student had to pass in the first semester. One encouragement he had came from passing English on his first try, which was made possible by the brilliant coaching of Paul Birch, a team member of AE from Vancouver. Another encouragement was passing Hebrew after he had decided to postpone the examination.

Because she really believed in prayer, Emily fasted and prayed while Ebe was away preaching. He never fasted as many days as she did before she became ill in Canada and had to take medication with her food.

V

TEACHING AND PREACHING

Ebe enjoyed countless opportunities to teach and do evangelism during school breaks. One such invitation came from missionary friends of the Free Methodist Church at Edwaleni, who invited him to speak at a youth camp. The date unexpectedly coincided with the birth of his and Emily's twin boys. One twin was in an incubator for a number of days, and it looked as if Ebe would not be able to speak at the camp. A couple of days before the start of the camp, he called the missionary, Elmore Clyde, and his wife Arlene, warning them of his dilemma. It was just about impossible for them to find a replacement. Ebe asked the doctors when Emily and the babies might be discharged. They gave him a late date. They could let them out only if Ebe would sign and assume the responsibility. They prayed and trusted the Lord. Ebe signed the discharge forms. Emily and the babies came home to the rousing, enthusiastic, and curious welcome

of their three older siblings, all two years apart. And coura-
geous Emily again assured her husband that she would manage, the Lord helping her. He left for Edwaleni.

Getting off the bus, he was driven to the mission station,
which was by then teeming with enthusiastic, energetic, excited, and praying young people. They watched the car out-
running the cloud of its own dust as it raced down a steep
mountain to a valley two miles or so away. As they drove up to
the mission's gate, the kids had formed a tremendous guard of
honour—to welcome him! Ebe said he felt so small that he
wanted to crawl under the carpet. Their enthusiastic singing
moved him profoundly. That youth camp was one of a kind. It
was uniquely blessed by the Lord.

The Free Methodist missionaries had discovered Ebenezer
through an unfortunate situation. Pastor William Duma, a
famous Baptist minister in Durban, regularly spoke at the Free
Methodist youth camps held every July. But this time he was
not going to be available and the missionaries learned of this
very late. Reverend Bernard Johanson, the principal of the Union Bible Institute (U.B.I.), was asked whether or not he could
speak in Duma's place. If not, could he suggest anyone he
might know that he could recommend to them? Johanson recommended Ebe. Ebe was well accepted by the campers. He
was younger and related well to them. From then on, he was
almost regularly invited to speak not only at youth camps and
their church conferences in South Africa, but years later also in
the United States.

There were several other invitations like these from other
churches and mission stations. He was booked nearly solidly

during vacations, long weekends, and other Christian events. These were costly to his family, but rewarding in other ways, including crucial financial support.

The fact that he was lecturing at the well-known U.B.I. opened up many opportunities for Ebenezer to teach and preach all around Natal, and even to other provinces and countries in Southern Africa. Here are some examples:

Conference at Fairview Mission Station

This was an old Free Methodist mission station with lots of educated people.

It had a well-known high school and primary school. It had had some soundly evangelical pastors in the past, but new younger missionaries had now come from the United States who were shaking things up in the church, which had become quite complacent over the years. They talked about a Reverend Cele, who had died and had been highly regarded as an excellent pastor. In fact, one distinguished gentleman who came to Christ during Ebe's meetings was the son of that pastor. He told Ebe that he had actually repented at his dad's graveside. He could not believe as a young man that his dad was really being buried and that his voice had been silenced for good. The convention went well and a good number of people made commitments to Jesus and rededicated their lives to Him.

Elmore Clyde and Warren Johnson were the new missionaries who had invited Ebe. They had come fresh from seminary with their young wives, fresh vision, and belief in fervent prayer. They each had a blue Chevrolet, so identical that even their ignition keys opened each other's cars. Ebe discovered this when he was given one of these cars to drive to the venue from the home where he was staying. That was the first time Ebe was trusted by a missionary with his car! Commitment to prayer for those young missionaries was very real. They did not just believe in prayer—they actually prayed. There is a difference between just believing something and actually carrying it through. They challenged the young prospective leadership of the church, some of whom were Ebe's students at U.B.I., to join in commitment to prayer every morning, and early! They demonstrated total dependence on the Lord. They were expecting and experiencing a revival.

Mqanduli Baptist Church

A gifted Baptist pastor invited Ebe to a church in the Transkei. The superintendent of that area was Reverend Phipson, an English man who spoke isiXhosa fluently. Ebe did not speak that language fluently, but it was similar enough to isiZulu that he did not need an interpreter. The church had many young people, and there were many more outside the church still to be brought into the fold. Since Ebe was still young, his ministry appealed to that young generation. In fact, a number of outsiders were brought in and a few of them even committed to the ministry and went to Union Bible Institute for training. U.B.I. was getting to be known as probably the best Bible School in Southern Africa at the time. A number of denominations were meeting with the principal, expressing their desire to send their prospective pastors to U.B.I., including some independent churches.

Lusikisiki Mission Hospital

This hospital was a long drive from U.B.I. The road was not paved. In fact, some parts of it were just two-wheel grooves with grass in the centre of the road. The amazing thing was that the South Africa Railway (SAR) buses owned by the government ran on those kinds of roads. The reason was, of course, that they were transporting black people who lived in the remote parts of their homelands. And the government was making lots of money. Some of the drivers of such buses were very rough and rude whites whose jobs were protected under the Job Reservation Act. Blacks were allowed to drive their own buses only after the government were seen to be seriously implementing their "Separate Development Policy." Another contributing factor to relaxing such Job Reservation hardships was the heating up of freedom fighters on the borders of South Africa. It became a serious risk to have whites travel deep into black territories where their safety could not be assured.

There were some people in the neighbourhood of the hospital who genuinely understood the Gospel. But there were those who were committed to Christianity merely as a religion. Their understanding of the Gospel was fuzzy. Methodism had been rooted in the Cape and Transkei by early missionaries, but many people had lost it. That was how it was in the Lusikisiki Hospital area. Some had been brought up well in Christian homes, understanding Christian principles but having no relationship with Christ. Every generation needs to be evangelized. Someone once said, "God has no grandchildren. They have to hear the Gospel, believe in Christ, and then become God's children."

VI
EVANGELIZING WITH AFRICAN ENTERPRISE (1970-1978)

Michael Cassidy

Michael was born in Johannesburg, South Africa. His parents, originally from Great Britain, met in Johannesburg and got married there. They moved to Lesotho where Michael grew up. He was educated in the best private schools in South Africa and Cambridge University in England. While attending the latter, he was led to Christ by a friend, a law student who was attending Billy Graham's crusade. He later entered Fuller Theological Seminary with a deep desire to transform not only his country, which was ravaged by apartheid, but the whole continent of Africa. "Evangelizing the cities of Africa through word and deed, in partnership with the church," was an idea conceived at Fuller. With the incredible interest shown by Dr. Charles Fuller, the president, in Michael's proposal, the organization of African Enterprise came into existence. There are now ten teams in Africa doing stratified evangelism in Africa.

Mission to Maritzburg

This was the first African Enterprise evangelistic mission held in Pietermaritzburg, in August of 1962. It was held in the city hall—thus African Enterprise made a crack in apartheid by allowing this first interracial gathering.

Ebe was a lecturer at Union Bible Institute. Ebe did a lot of translating in isiZulu for visiting speakers at the Institute. Some of the U.B.I. students studied in English, and others in isiZulu. So it was necessary to translate chapel messages preached in English. Some of these distinguished speakers included the former president of Moody Bible Institute, the Bishop of the Free Methodist Church, and Dr. Ted Engstrom of World Vision International.

One morning, he found himself translating for a young man who was a student at Fuller Theological Seminary in Pasadena, California. The man's name was Michael Cassidy. He was destined to become the founder of AE. He was a very winsome young man who had a great sense of humour when describing his vision. Michael and Ebe hit it off right away. And when he finished speaking and left the chapel, he showed a lot of interest in Ebe and stopped to chat with him. This was unusual. He noticed that Michael made notes in his diary as they talked. Ebe was not aware that he was unsuspectingly be-

36

coming a "marked man." This was as far back as 1961. Word went around that Michael and his group would be coming back to hold an evangelistic mission in Pietermaritzburg (called "Mission to Maritzburg"). These missions were usually called "revivals" in South Africa. Michael was informing faculty and students of this, as well as preaching a pungent Gospel message. Students were very interested and hoped to see in him another evangelist in the stature of Billy Graham, or Nicholas Bhengu.

The planning stages became serious in 1961. By 1962, preparations for this "revival" coming to Pietermaritzburg were in full swing. It was to be held in the city hall, and the AE office was secured diagonally across from it. Some of the messages were to be translated into isiZulu, because non-English speaking blacks were to be allowed into the city hall! Wow! Michael was looking for a translator. Because of their initial meeting, Ebe was called upon to fill that important role. It was felt that even some excellent court translators could not handle theological terms. It was for that same reason that Ebe was called upon when Billy Graham preached at a Durban stadium in 1973, and when Jim Erwin, the astronaut who walked on the moon, spoke at the Mariannhill Stadium in 1974. Michael had a hand in all of these situations. That was how Ebe ended up with he interesting role as translator and director of a black male voice choir, the first ever to sing in the Pietermaritzburg City Hall.

The chairman of the Mission to Maritzburg Committee was Dr. Archie Hart.

He was the city engineer, and did a superb job of working with the committee.

Archie was also the emcee during the mission, during which Ebe got to know him. Little did he know that this gentleman would do something very significant for the Edendale Township. When Ebe was planning to build his family's home in Edendale, he was denied two things. The Natal Building Society would not give him a loan, because under apartheid it was illegal to do so. The second thing was electricity. He could not have electricity in his house. No African family had electricity. Townships had lights for streets at night only, to enable the police to chase "Black rascals." There were no domestic cables to deliver electricity during the day. Ebe visited Archie and asked if there was any chance of getting a domestic cable installed. Archie got it installed in no time. Consequently, many homes were granted electricity. In fact, it was amusing to see a couple of houses built of wattle and daub with electric bulbs shining in their homes. This is also an example of how some people found ways around the strict laws legislated against blacks.

Mission to Maritzburg brought many significant professional people to Christ, to say nothing of the ordinary citizens of Pietermaritzburg. It seemed to put a seal of approval to the ministry of the young AE organization. This was the beginning of a relationship with African Enterprise which is now in its fifth decade. Ebe both translated for Michael, and began to preach in townships where it was not possible to hold interracial meetings. The Mission to Ladysmith was one such example where AE could not hold an interracial mission. Even though the team was committed to holding racially mixed meetings, they hit a stone wall in this predominantly Afrikaans-speaking city of Ladysmith. They had to set up segregated meetings that ran concurrently in the white suburb and the black township. Michael was given special permission to preach in the township just outside Ladysmith.

There were no major problems holding integrated meetings in many other evangelistic missions, yet there were many strategic situations where it was just not possible to hold mixed meetings. Apartheid was so effective in segregating people that it would have been pointless to move groups of people to a venue that would allow integration. It made more sense to go to where people were and to make meetings accessible to each community. Hence the Stratified Evangelism concept that AE came up with—reaching people where they are.

Mission '70

Ebe joined AE officially on January 1, 1970 when a major mission that lasted a whole year began in Johannesburg. Attempting to evangelize a large city like that was an ambitious project. Ebe directed the Zulu ministry in the neighbouring township of Soweto. They had an office there and a good number of staff members. When they arrived in Johannesburg, Ebe discovered that his family was not allowed to reside in the province then called Transvaal. They were virtually ordered back to Natal because they were foreigners from another province of South Africa. That was apartheid! It was only through a long, drawn-out process and the skilful negotiation of John Rees,

Chair of Mission '70, that they were finally allowed to live and work in Johannesburg. There were special conditions attached to the permit that they had to meet. Rees was only successful in resolving the protracted debate to send Ebe and his family back to Natal because John was white. Not only that, but he was a high-ranking official in the so-called Bantu City Administration in Johannesburg. Even though Michael was white, no one would have listened to him. So Rees was qualified to work and secure the permit for the Sikakanes. In fact, he succeeded in getting the powers that be to reverse the order they had already given that Ebe should be on his bike back to Natal.

There were many instances during this mission that indicated how apartheid was making peoples lives intolerable in South Africa. One day, several mixed AE team members left the office to catch a train from Pietermaritzburg to Johannesburg. At the railway station, they had to split down according to colour lines. White members moved to "Whites Only" compartments. Abiel and Ebe went to "their" compartments with "all-wood sofas" to sleep on throughout the night while the other guys went to their green leather sofas that converted into beds as night.

Apart from the government red tape, Ebe was nearly killed by criminal "tsotsies" one evening. He was following a car that suddenly veered off to the left. Ebe soon noticed that the reason its driver acted so strangely was that he had seen two guys dressed up like traffic police flagging him down to stop. Ebe realized that they were robbers. No traffic police car was to be seen there. There was no room for him to veer off and no room to reverse. Ebe simply put his foot on the gas and went straight towards the guy on his side. The guy knew he was a goner! He quickly gave way, thus enabling Ebe to escape. The following morning, papers reported that those same guys had actually killed one man at a similar "hold-up" in another part of Soweto.

AE, together with participating ministers and churches, left a fairly good mark on Johannesburg that year. They started seeing converts from the very beginning—even at the pre-mission phase—in meetings held in churches, schools, and public gatherings. Ebe remembered a respected lady physician who represented her church at the training of counsellors who was transformed, and bore a clear testimony of how Christ spoke to her and how she had yielded her life to Him. Wherever they ministered, there were good results.

Back to Pietermaritzburg

Team members took some vacation after the year of gruelling activity in Johannesburg and before they returned to their base, Pietermaritzburg. Ebe and his family took a long drive to Cape Town via the beautiful Garden Route. They visited some friends and some places of interest, like going up to Table Mountain via cable. They also visited Groote Schuur Hospital, where the world's first heart transplant was performed by Dr. Christiaan Barnard. Then, they went to the very spot where the former Prime Minister of South Africa, the architect of apartheid, Dr. Hendrik Verwoerd, was stabbed three times by Dimitrio Tsafendas, who was a parliamentary messenger. This had happened on September 16, 1966. Ten years later, on

June 16, 1976, the black youth political uprising that was perhaps the beginning of the toppling of apartheid was sparked off in Soweto.

After regrouping back in Maritzburg, it felt so good and refreshing to handle smaller situations that were manageable without elaborate preparations and planning. Some churches in the city were approached to see if they could give AE opportunities to minister to people working in the city. A good example of this happened at the cathedral right in the city's centre. Lunch hour meetings were advertised that would take place at the cathedral. A series of films were shown once a week. These were not all evangelistic. Some were educational, showing Armstrong landing on the moon; some were dealing with health issues; some were Moody Science films; and, of course, some had a clear message of the Gospel. Small AE teams got into factories, farms, schools, hospitals, colleges, and universities. These ministries were happening while small town missions were being negotiated, prayed for, planned, and executed. You got the feeling that the world to evangelize and conquer was not only far way, but right before you and within reach. AE became a beehive of activity. People were coming in and going out. Team members were becoming busier and busier.

Problems in African Education

One day, Ebe had a chat with Mrs. Zama, the wife of a school inspector. She was terribly unhappy with the problems faced by black schools in South Africa, and particularly around

42

KwaZulu-Natal. There were not enough schools for children, and so children were sent back home at the opening of each school year. They had to have money for uniforms, books, the building fund, and other requirements as a pre-condition for admission. Education was not free for blacks. Whites had free and compulsory education. The government budget was enough for paying teachers' salaries and some other expenses, but they would not build schools. Feeling very strongly about this, Ebe discussed it with the AE team, who gave him the green light to go ahead and pursue any avenues available to him. The first thing he did was to make an appointment with the mayor of Pietermaritzburg. They met in his city hall parlour and discussed how money could be raised to meet the need of building schools. The mayor happened to be a Christian who worshipped in the Baptist Church, and was very sympathetic. Ebe then proceeded to find a couple of white business men. The two leading members of the committee were Mr. Norman and Mr. Nash. They formed a committee after several meetings. An article went to the local paper. They asked donors to deposit donations in the chosen bank. The name of the organization was Zulu Education and Teaching Assistance (ZETA). When they registered ZETA, they found that Ebe could not be a member of the committee because he was black. He was told that he could only sit in as an observer! Once again, that was apartheid for you! That was how they got away with that restriction.

They raised money to start building the first high school. Ebe consulted Inspector P.P. Zama concerning the best area to build this first school. Zama was pleased to advise, and in fact it was Zama who named the first school, Amakholwa High School. Amakholwa means "Christians." Mr. Zama was a committed Christian who was a key member of his church, the Salvation Army. The next high school was called Laduma High School. This endeavour resulted in a number of other high schools being built around Pietermaritzburg. It was one of many contributions that Ebe and AE made to the black community. It was in keeping with the ministry of AE to assist communities in practical ways.

It transpired that the member of the city council appointed by the mayor to be in charge of schools was a racist. He was the one who handled the budget to improve education for Urban Bantu, but he scuttled and strangled any attempts to do so. Meanwhile, he would give good reports to council. Blacks who met with him were obviously frustrated with him, yet he was known to be a faithful member of his mainstream denomination.

VII
MOVING BEYOND
SOUTH AFRICA

Nairobi in Kenya

The first country that Ebe visited outside South Africa was Kenya. The AE team had completed Mission '70 in Johannesburg when Ebe went to Kenya and stayed with Dr. Don Jacobs. It was quite an experience for him to see a free black state where black people were completely in charge. Everything was controlled and run by them. Ebe had followed the news regarding the Mau-Mau uprising in Kenya. Such news had a very "white twist" to it. Being there gave Ebe another side of the story as well. He met whites in Nairobi who were happy with change though acknowledging the violence it took to bring about the change. One Kenyan showed the scars he bore on his body. Ebe was taken to the street where the popular Tom Mboya had been assassinated. The bullet marks were still there for tourists to see. There was also the problem of unemployment. Young adults, Ebe was told, flocked to the city of Nairobi from rural areas with the hope of netting jobs and making a good living for themselves. However, there were no jobs for many of them. This resulted in the erection of shacks, an influx of prostitutes, and everything else that goes with that.

It was amazing for Ebe, coming from apartheid South Africa, to meet and talk to Kenyan youth who did not seem to even know what the Mau-Mau uprising in Kenya was all about. That was unlike the South African youth, who were the same age and bitter about apartheid. When Ebe and Emily visited the new South Africa after the dismantling of apartheid, they saw the same thing there, too. The bitter spirit of the young people who sparked off the uprising in Soweto on June 16, 1976, which ultimately led to the collapse of apartheid, was no longer evident. They saw black and white students walking together from a formerly all-white high school in Newcastle, now integrated, joking and giggling as though life had always been like that. The Zulu Canadian couple— Ebe and Emily—could not believe their eyes. When they had escaped to Canada, they had never expected to see that in their lifetime.

Ivory Coast

Ivory Coast was one of the many countries that Ebe visited. On this occasion, he teamed up with John Wilson from the AE team based in Uganda. They were invited to lead workshops and leadership training of a group of thirty young pastors. The conference was held just outside Abidjan, the capital of Ivory Coast (Cote D'Ivoire) at the time. It was sponsored by the Alliance Church. There were several churches participating in the conference. We learned upon arrival that Ivory Coast President Felix Houphouet-Boigny was Roman Catholic. He apparently subsidized Roman Catholic conferences. So the organizers of the evangelical conference appealed to the president to subsidize their conference because it was their taxes that subsidized Roman Catholic gatherings. And he did!

The thing that impressed visitors the most was seeing the calibre of the pastors who attended. The average age would have been about 25. They seemed to be soundly grounded in the Word and showed a genuine desire to serve the Lord. Stories shared from their experience in the ministry indicated this fact. John and Ebe took turns leading the sessions and interacting with pastors. It was a very fulfilling time. The church service they attended on the Sunday they were there was a good size congregation and the worship was very uplifting. The choir wore colourful African gowns not cut like western ones. They sang mainly national tunes.

The heat was intense in that part of the country. The Ivorian hosts provided John Wilson and Ebe with some air conditioners, which helped a great deal, especially at night. John and Ebe took a long bus trip to the small village of Yamoussoukro, where the president was born. He was preparing to move the capital from the large city of Abidjan to his "small village." The new capital was under construction at the time. An Israeli company of architects had been hired to design this modern city from scratch. Israelis were doing it all. The

Houses of Parliament and the city hall had been constructed, and they were something to behold. Nobody had ever seen such wide roads in Africa before!

Incidentally, this was Ebe's second visit to Ivory Coast. The first one had nearly been a disaster. Before flying to Abidjan from Pasadena, he had gone to Washington D.C. and rounded up several West African embassies to secure visas to enter their countries. As he was traveling on a South African passport, he was carefully scrutinized by embassies in Washington D.C., because as the Nigerian High Commissioner had put it, emphasizing each word, "Why would the South African government give *you* a passport?" The question implied that they thought he was probably a collaborator or government stooge. Some countries like Sierra Leone simply refused him a visa. Even Kenya, where he had been allowed a couple of times previously, turned down his visa application. The purpose of his trip to West Africa was to explore the possibility of an AE team there.

Ebe's flight arrived ahead of schedule in Abidjan. This meant that Ebe had to go through customs without the aid of Dr. Zoukoe and a missionary friend, who were to be his hosts. It became unbearable. The customs officials spoke only French, and when they saw his South African passport, they would not allow him entry. Ebe tried to explain through a would-be translator that the visa had been issued by their country's embassy in Washington D.C. The response was that the embassy should have checked with the head office in Abidjan before issuing it.

48

In addition to Ebe, there were four other culprits who were escorted like criminals to some office for questioning. Ebe never found out where the other guys came from and what they were questioned about. They spoke no English. They were kept in a waiting room and Ebe was third in line. To their right was a heavy glass door. It looked half an inch thick. Age had taken its toll on it. This obscure glass looked badly scratched. They sat quietly and could barely hear the sounds of people talking behind the door. The first guy emerged from the interrogation handcuffed and accompanied by some junior official.

The second guy was let into the office. While he was questioned, Dr. Zokoue stepped into the waiting room before the interrogation was complete. Ebe was extremely relieved, because Zokoue would at least know his whereabouts after the ordeal if they landed him in jail. Ebe and Zokoue talked briefly before the glass door opened. The guy was led out. During Ebe's questioning, Zokoue became his advocate, speaking in French. Then he took Ebe out to the white missionary who was with him. This friend of his had just taken a jolly ride with him to the airport. But God had a purpose in that. Zokoue said that the officials wanted him to take Ebe down to the head office in the city.

They drove down and sat in the lounge awaiting the arrival of the "big official." Eventually, the elevator door opened. A pleasant, good looking, youngish executive came out. He took a look at them, and with one quick look at the missionary, he jumped to him, saying, "Bob, what brings you here, brother?" They hugged each other and chatted about the ministry. That was the end of Ebe's criminal offense! That was God's purpose for bringing Bob to the airport. My papers casually got the signature they needed after the official listened briefly but with interest to Ebe's South African story, which even Zokoue didn't know. That was the end of his ordeal!

New York City

John Wilson was an AE team member based in Uganda, his home country. He was a big business man—a former executive of a major oil company in Uganda. He and Ebe went to speak at the first Black Congress on Evangelism in New York City, sponsored by the then well-known and eloquent Tom Skinner. It was held in one of the big hotels in New York City. It was not a huge affair but was attended by some well-selected, strategically targeted African Americans. John and Ebe shared the ministry there, as they always did. They had become partners in the ministry, just as Michael Cassidy was with Bishop Festo Kivengere.

New York was an overwhelming city. When Ebe first visited the city with Chris Smith, entering it by car, there was an unsettling, eerie atmosphere that could not be explained. It was an old looking part of the city, with buildings of red brick, covered with disturbing graffiti. It was obviously a poverty-stricken part of the city. But John and Ebe got to the city centre where there were people everywhere—people, people, too many people! Some elite people were lining up to buy tickets to get into some show. They saw four lines of people stretching a couple of blocks deep. Trains were congested with people.

The yellow cabs were everywhere on streets jammed with traffic. No wonder a gentleman who took these African speakers for a jolly ride from the Congress Hotel so they could see some residential areas of New York got lost. He took them through rows and rows of joined buildings (they refer to them as *trains* in South Africa), and he was about to pinpoint the house where he was picking up a couple to take them to the conference when he discovered that he was in a totally different part of the city—identical to the one he was looking for.

The congress sessions went well. AE ministry missions was featured prominently, specially who they were and how they conducted evangelism. Their focus on evangelism in the cities of Africa was important to the Americans, who wanted to know how they were dealing with alarming issues of poverty and needs. Ebe and his group wanted to examine how their approach might be different or similar to the needs of American inner cities. Apartheid was at its height in South Africa and of great challenge to African Americans in the United States. The issues generated great discussions that were very profitable. The consensus was to free Africa with all her problems and challenges. A great deal of time was devoted to reaching children, as there were a good number of Sunday School teachers in the congress, teachers who were partners in sponsoring the congress.

Omaha in Nebraska

Ebe went to speak at a church in Omaha, Nebraska. He was met at the airport by his host, a Marine who was in his full, impressive uniform. This was during the time when there was a big general meeting of the UN in New York. Airports were carrying a lot of world dignitaries from all over the world. The officer who met Ebe picked up his suitcase and carried it for him while he carried his briefcase. As they were walking through the airport to cross the road towards the parking lot, about three security people ran ahead of them and stopped all the traffic and people, clearing the way for this little AE dignitary, mistaken for a UN official guest.

Zimbabwe Pastors' Conference

The AE team flew in a small plane to the neighbouring country of Zimbabwe (formerly Rhodesia) and landed in the city called Salisbury (now Harare). This was right in the middle of that country's war of independence. There was some uneasiness as they flew over the unoccupied parts of the country where the war was happening, because the small aircraft could have been brought down very easily!

As expected, the team ran into a very tense situation in Zimbabwe. It was not easy to talk *reconciliation* between God's servants, black and white pastors. Their white sons were dying trying to seal the borders in defence of the country; the other's black sons were dying trying to take back their country. The atmosphere was extremely thick. You could "cut it with a knife." There did not seem to have been any dialogue between black and white pastors. The conference spent a whole week opening the Word and trying to make it relevant to their situation, because it *was* relevant. There were extended times of prayer together. No significant breakthrough seemed to be forthcoming, though. There were agreements made with Scripture as they saw their role as pastors serving in such a polarized nation. They discussed the situation as realistically as possible. Pastors were strongly challenged to be part of the solution instead of being part of the problem. It was true to say that the tension was beginning to lessen as the week progressed, and it seemed as if things were moving the right direction. Pastors living in close proximity were encouraged to get together interracially and pray for the country's problems and for each other and to recognize their divine role as representatives of God's Kingdom. The importance of the body of Christ to be part of the solution instead of being part of the problem was really emphasized.

The final meeting was supposed to strike a high note of victorious praise. It turned out to be a near disaster. The summary of what the conference was about had been outlined to the visitors who joined the conference. An all-white church choir had sung. It would have been appropriate to bring in an interracial choir. And for the final prayer, the emcee asked a white gentleman who was singing in the choir to close in prayer. The team members from apartheid South Africa were already uneasy. They had nothing to do with that crucial programme. They would have liked to see a mixed choir joining in singing, even a simple well-known hymn of praise. Fingers were crossed throughout the service. The white emcee then asked a choir member to lead in a closing prayer. Well! That was an unfortunate choice. He unwittingly called on someone who came in cold to the meeting, and was not fully aware of what was going on, and what had transpired during the week. He prayed a prayer that was probably prayed in some white churches. He called on God to destroy all these evil people on their borders who were disturbing their peaceful country! You can understand what that did, undoing all that had been built up during the week. It simply infuriated black pastors whose sons were fighting from outside the country.

Michael Cassidy, Phineas Dube, and rest of the African Enterprise team worked till the small hours of the morning with those who had stayed on, praying and mending the relationships with those who accepted Michael's pleas to stay behind after the meeting was dismissed. They worked and even used what had happened to point out the importance and need for sensitivity. Some of them were understandably frustrated and discouraged. The conference ended on a less than victorious note, even though some pastors really understood where the man who prayed was coming from. The need for reconciliation was realized in a new way.

Ebe returned home with some mixed feelings, upset and discouraged. The following morning, he was asked to join Michael Cassidy at a press conference held in Durban. It was all on their trip to Zimbabwe. When they returned from Durban, he learned before he got home that their house in Edendale had been broken into. Emily had returned home early from the school where she taught. She found their house surrounded by their few disbelieving neighbours. She had to drive right back to the police station to report the "burglary." Before she got inside the office, one of the black officials asked her if she was the lady from the house that had been broken into.

She wondered how he knew that. Anyway, she entered the office to make a statement. The officer who spoke to her was very casual. He asked her to return home and that they would be following her to lift fingerprints. No one ever came.

Everyone's thinking was that the house had been broken into by thieves. But that was not to be. Police had posed as thieves. The whole thing bore clear marks of being the work of the police. They searched through Ebe's still unpacked suitcase, which he had taken to Zimbabwe. They removed a file that had notes Ebe had used in Zimbabwe. They took John Stott's cassette tape and went into their son's bedroom, plugged his cassette player into the wall, and listened to it. Stott was a suspect of the government because he seemed to associate somehow with the World Council of Churches. But he was not involved with that organization, which was very critical of apartheid. The South African government hated it. And finally, the "burglars" had gone into the refrigerator and broke all the ice in the freezer. We learned something we'd never heard of before, that subversive documents could be wrapped up in plastics and hidden in the freezer!

Astronaut Jim Erwin

This name may not be known to some readers, but Jim Erwin is a man who actually landed on the moon—walked on it and then returned to earth again. He became a celebrity the day he returned.

Michael Cassidy managed to schedule an unusual evangelistic thrust with Jim Erwin. A big stadium was booked in

Marianhill outside Durban. The one day meeting was publicized widely, and the stadium was packed with curious people who wanted to see someone who had been to the moon! The diminutive scientist carried and displayed rock samples he had brought back from the moon. He declared that it was "great for a man to walk on the moon, but it was greater for God to walk on the earth—Jesus the Incarnate God, the Son." With Ebe translating for him, he gave clear testimony of his relationship with the Lord Jesus. And he gave a powerful message of the Gospel. Many came forward to surrender to the Lord who was incarnated, and actually walked on the earth seeking the lost, who died on the cross to save them from their sins.

VIII

SCHOOL OF
WORLD MISSIONS

Ebe was one of a few team members whom African Enterprise sent to study at Fuller Theological Seminary's School of World Mission. Each team member took his family with him. The decision was made that all of Ebe's seven family members would begin preparations to go the United States. Ebe was wondering if the opportunity to leave South Africa at that particular time would ultimately lead to being posted in Canada as a representative for African Enterprise, not a director. He had already discussed the possibility of moving to Canada with Ken and Hazel Wardle. That couple had left a large church in Pietermaritzburg and gone to Canada because they did not want their children to grow up in apartheid South Africa. For Ebe's big family, the deposit for their passports was going to cost $2,800. But African Enterprise found that if the deposit needed for blacks to go abroad was guaranteed by a church, it could be waived. So, African Enterprise guaranteed it because they were a Christian organization. By May 1976, all their passports were secured. But a new problem surfaced. Because of a bad financial crunch that year, the women in Pasadena who were responsible for raising funds could not raise full support for all of them by the time Ebe was to start summer school.

So Ebe and Emily had to depart, leaving their children behind. It was difficult for them to leave, especially for Emily, because their son Ben was one of the four students chosen at random to stand trial on behalf of the rest of the students arrested in the wake of the Soweto uprising of 1976. He was at the University of the North (in Turfloop).

When they arrived in Pasadena, they were welcomed warmly by the AE staff and by Friendship Baptist Church. People from Friendship met them at the airport and had dinner with them in a lovely hotel. Then they temporarily went to the apartment before going on into a house on Los Robles Avenue near the Fuller Book Store.

That was the beginning of a busy time spent studying, researching, and writing assignments. There was a lot to learn. Living and mixing with white people all day long, day after day, was a new and incredible thing for people from South Africa. An AE staff member took them to Disneyland. What a sight that was for Emily, who was there for the first time. They met a friend from Swaziland in Disneyland—Abraham Xaba and his American wife. He had met her when he was studying at Westmount College. You would think that the chances of finding one person you knew from Swaziland were one in a million considering the thousands of people milling around Disneyland.

They found Americans to be very friendly and open in ways they had not experienced in South Africa. Friendship Baptist church's senior pastor, and his congregation, overwhelmed them with their hospitality and love. Opportunities to share their faith, share about AE, and preach were always there for them. On January 1, they experienced an astounding demonstration of American hospitality. This was not just the first day of the year, but a day of watching the fabulous Rose Parade, which was a huge celebration. And it coincided with Ebe's birthday, which was usually overshadowed by big Christmas events. Ebe and Emily were told to spend a relaxed night on December 31. Their hosts were going to take chairs and place them at the best point along the Rose Parade from where they would be able to see the gorgeous floats in view for the longest possible time. A certain gentleman had offered to be at that point to place their chairs, and those of their friends who would be with them. He would spend the whole night there ensuring that no one interfered with that strategically selected spot. That was exactly what happened. They watched those floats beautifully and artistically covered with an incredible array of flowers. Trained bands sang and marched flawlessly to the beat of the music and drums. Horse riders were a trotting down the street in perfect sync.

WRESTLING WITH APARTHEID

Beverly Hills Lawyers

At Fuller Theological Seminary, Ebe was completing his master's degree in theology, and Emily took some courses at the Pasadena Community College, which was very nearby to Fuller Seminary. Before graduating, he had another rub with the apartheid regime. He got an invitation to speak to seventy lawyers in Beverley Hills. This was one of the usual things... invitations to speak here, there, and thither! These lawyers had been given the assignment of reviewing the United States foreign policy towards South Africa. This came about as the result of former President Gerald Ford losing to Governor Jimmy Carter. Ebe had no idea as to how on earth they had ever heard about him, But the invitation came asking for him to speak on the subject of "The Violation of Human Rights in South Africa." He left Fuller quite early, making some allowance for the possibility of getting lost at night. Sure enough, he was a couple of minutes late.

The meeting was held in a large house. All seventy lawyers fitted comfortably in the lounge. The chairman met the speaker and introduced him to the frightening, august gathering. He joyfully introduced him to a "fellow South African" who was the Head of the South Africa Information Service! A lady who was his chauffer was also introduced. Ebe's blood pressure and heartbeat skyrocketed. He was visibly shaken. He could not share in the food that was provided. He couldn't. He gradually calmed down and regained his composure. Eventually, he asked to have a word with the chairman. He asked him if he realized what it would mean for him and his future to speak on the subject in the presence of the director of the South Africa Information Service. He spoke about hearing the two sides of the story. It had been rumoured that this man's Information department had offered a big reward for anyone who would kill one of the homeland leaders who had refused to accept "independence" for his homeland. Ebe wasn't sure about that. It simply scared the wits out of him to present the information to the very person who, among other things, was being paid to get that very information for his government.

The chairman had not thought of this. He wondered if he should send the speaker back home. Ebe said there was no way the matter could be resolved. Ebe would have had to explain why he was leaving. He could not change his talk either, and say things the director would want to hear. The information would be in South Africa the following morning. And what would *blacks* think of him? He'd be a real candidate for what they called a "burning necklace." For the blacks would find those who "sold out" to the whites and adorn them with a rubber tire around his neck, filled with gas, and set it alight! It was a no-win situation.

Ebe gave his talk as he had prepared it. From the brief interaction he had with this "fellow South African," Ebe was almost certain that the man was a Coloured. That was the official category given by the government denoting one who was neither white nor black, but of mixed race. He was pretty close to being blonde. He read his paper, justifying apartheid, which had undoubtedly been prepared by an expert back in Pretoria, to be used anywhere he was invited to speak. Ebe listened intently. One illustration in the paper concerned the humiliation of Coloureds, their brothers and sisters who were classified as non-whites. Ebe pretended not to know that the man speaking was Coloured. Some Coloured left the Cape and moved north to Johannesburg. There, they posed as whites. They moved into white areas, got a white job, a white salary, and enrolled their children in white schools. If they were discovered by the standing Commission of Inquiry into people's genealogies, then they forfeited all these privileges and were sent out to "Noordgesig," their Coloured area, which the Group Areas policy had assigned to them. Many of those South African people had chosen to commit suicide rather than suffer that kind of humiliation. Ebe turned to his "fellow South African," looked him straight in the eye, and said, "I believe that he will bear me out because he must have heard of some of these cases."

The most amusing episode of the evening came during the question and answer period. The director did not do very well under some gentle attacks. Most of the questions were sympathetic to the cause of black people. His chauffer was furious when she came up with a question in defence of her boss, which was directed at Ebe. She basically said, "The reason President Ford lost the election is because lots of Americans have not mastered the art of voting for a government—how can you expect rural amaZulu to vote sensibly for a democratic government?"

Ebe shrugged this off by saying that if the American people had not learned it in all these centuries, then amaZulu might just as well join them as "fellow-fumblers" and not be expected to wait until Americans learned before they started the long process of learning to vote. Ebe wondered how Americans would feel about this criticism by one of their own. Obviously, some of the things Ebe said in that meeting about the evils of apartheid and the violation of human fights in South Africa were added to the file that the police had compiled on him in South Africa.

Panama

On their way back to South Africa from Fuller Seminary after Ebe's graduation, he and Emily stopped in a few places on behalf of AE. One of those was Panama. They were exploring possibilities for future evangelistic missions for AE. There was one contact in Panama who was interested in the ministry of AE. There was also Ebe's former student from the Ontario Bible College, who was a missionary to the Mestizo people in Panama. There were a couple of opportunities for them to share their testimonies and contact some key people who might be in a position to invite in the AE team. The prospects were not very good, the main stumbling block for them being finances to fund such a mission, and there were no later opportunities to stage a mission in Panama.

One interesting thing that stood out in their minds was a visit to the Panama Canal to see the locks and be shown the fascinating process of how ships were moved from the water level of the Atlantic Ocean to that of the Pacific Ocean. Water from the lower ocean was raised up to the level of the other ocean so that the ship was able to sail through the canal to its destination. From Panama, Emily flew to Johannesburg through Rio de Janeiro, Brazil while Ebe flew to Washington D.C. to obtain visas for some countries in West Africa. He encountered some difficulties because he was traveling on the South African passport, which was boycotted by and unacceptable in most African countries.

Malawi Keswick Convention

Blantyre was still the capital of Malawi. This was the only time Ebe was ever invited to be a speaker at any of the worldwide network of Keswick Christian conventions. Founded in England, the movement was known for having especially gifted speakers. It was a greatly challenging time for him. The invitation came as a complete surprise. Anyway, he flew up to Blantyre. The meetings were very blessed by the Lord, who brought some people to Himself as they responded to the Gospel. Malawians were generally very responsive to the Gospel—very hospitable and receptive people, both adults and youth. The large youth rally that followed the convention was well attended for just the one evening.

Some twenty-four years later, a friend from Malawi told Ebe about his brother-in-law had been converted during those days. Also, when Ebe was teaching at Tyndale, a friend of his who worked for World Vision based in Newmarket brought the director of World Vision in Malawi to speak at Ebe's missions class. Ebe had never seen her before. Her opening words went something like this: "Your professor doesn't know me. I know him. I was converted at the Malawi Keswick Convention when he spoke to the young people one evening." She went on to repeat his message in some details!

IX
RECONCILIATION MINISTRY

O ne of the most important emphases in the AE ministry is still reconciliation. No one could ever operate in the fragmented South Africa and ignore the urgent need for reconciliation there.

Ebe's Secretary

From day one, AE sought to practise what they preached. There were unwritten laws of the organization. The colour of someone's skin did not matter. When Ebe moved from Sweetwaters to work with African Enterprise, he was given an office just like the ones that white team members had. He was told he was to use the same toilet as was used by "Men." For the first time, he saw what a white sacred toilet looked like inside! He was given a secretary, a Dictaphone, and every privilege that everyone else had. In fact, when they gave him a white secretary, he was blown away. Actually, his first secretary came from an Afrikaans background, and she enjoyed being a secretary to a black man. She came to the office after one weekend and shared an amusing incident when her friends were discussing their workplaces. She shared about her good boss and ended up giving them his last name, which they understood to be umZulu. Some of her white friends were shocked and disappointed. She expected that.

Photographed With a White Lady

Preparing for a citywide mission in Pietermaritzburg, Ebe teamed up with a doctor's wife. Her husband was a highly respected Christian physician. He did not know and did not need to know how he ended up teaming up with her. Together with his AE colleagues, they set up a few teams to go to homes where they spoke at the ten o'clock tea meetings for ladies. The white Christian host would invite as many neighbours as she could get to come and hear the story of the mission being planned. The team members gave their testimonies and promoted the evangelistic mission coming to the city. Tea and cookies were served as discussions went on. Servers were black women employed in those homes.

Things were reversed on a number of occasions. Black women were invited into the white home and sat in the lounge while teams shared their testimonies and told them about the coming mission. At the end, they experienced something they had never ever seen before—they were served tea and cookies by their white employers! Ebe's team was visited by the media in one of these meetings who wrote a great story about AE bringing down the barriers in the city. The article was supported by a photograph in the Natal Witness, featuring the doctor's wife standing with Ebe. She was a wonderful Christian. It raised a few eyebrows. A few whites who knew AE made some encouraging comments.

Improving Work Conditions for Domestics

We had a very unique mission in Pietermaritzburg, which was not designed to hold a stadium series of evangelistic preaching. To be sure, there was a lot of witnessing and sharing of Christ's message, and people coming to Christ in the process. It was a mission that sought to improve the lot for the overlooked people in the society—the "nannies." *Nanny* was the name given to so-called "kitchen girls." Any black woman's name was Nanny. There were white employers who had the decency of calling them by their real names, while many more never bothered getting to know the first name of a woman who cooked their food. These nannies cared for their employers' most important treasure in the home—their children. They used the expressions "kitchen girls" and "garden boys." Every female was a "girl," regardless of her age. The male was a "boy," no matter how old he might have been.

Ebe said, "I remember when I was at a bank once and was asked to sit and wait for the manager outside his office. There was a little white boy sitting on the same bench waiting for his mother, who was queuing for the teller's service. The little boy was surprised that I had the nerve to sit on the same bench with him. So, he said to me 'Boy, what do you want here?' He was so scared when I asked him to repeat that. His mother came tearing into me, 'What are you saying to my son?' I said calmly, 'You ask him what he was saying to me.' After he told her, she turned to me and said, 'What should he call you if he does not know your name?' I infuriated her when I pointed at a white man in the queue who was about my age and said, 'Would he call that gentleman "boy" if he didn't know his name?'"

Back to so-called "kitchen girls." Rather than articulating the needs of this sector of society, AE sought support of different groups that were more influential and able to bring about change to the situation of domestic ladies. They met with groups of black ladies separately and listened to their side of the story. AE team members were shocked when they learned how much some nannies were paid. The questions of a minimum wage seemed to be "outrageous." They heard from a lady who was being paid less than her monthly bus fare. The question was asked why she continued to work for a household that paid her so little. She explained that if she left that job, and her employer signed her reference book ("Dom Pass," in Afrikaans), she would be sent out of the city and become a rural Bantu. She would be banned from ever entering the urban area again. She was trapped in a catch-22 situation.

Here is an illustration of what she was talking about. A white Christian lady who attended a Bible Study group arrived late one evening. She apologized profusely for being late. She had had to clean up after supper because she had fired her nanny. The reason was that her "girl" had taken dishes to clean up after supper and poured remaining tea into "their cup" and drank it. Her "Missus" burst into the kitchen unexpectedly. "Nanny! Who is going to drink out of that cup again?" The woman then smashed the cup and signed her reference book. She then ceased to be an urban Bantu. Ebe testified to the fact that many times he had been given tea in "jam tin cups" by white Christians and told to sit and drink it outside, or maybe under the veranda or in the kitchen. Tea in those converted jam containers was burning hot!

Conversely, they feared to be as brave as the late Dr. David Bosch, and his wife, still living, who brought black ministers into their dining room and served them dinner using their utensils. Their white Afrikaner neighbours eventually threw rocks through their windows and ostracized them.

Interracial Small Groups

One of the strategies that Cassidy came up with to work towards reconciliation in South Africa was the creation of small groups that were interracially mixed. We attended one in Edendale at a friend's house. These groups did not meet to have tea and talk about the weather. They grappled with the real issues of apartheid. The discussions were very frank and open. The groups that had a chance of surviving were those held in the white areas. It became unsafe to have whites come to a black township at night. It was also difficult for blacks to get into white suburbs. Transport was problematic for people who depended on public transportation, which was not available at night.

RECONCILIATION MINISTRY

Michael Cassidy, a Visionary

Michael was a man with very clear marks of a good leader. From the time he discussed the possibility of having Ebe join AE, he visualized clearly how he saw him fit into the organization and how that would expand and broaden his ministry. As they continued to work together, this became clearer. In Johannesburg's Mission '70, Ebe was appointed director of Zulu Ministries. Michael felt that Ebe would later assume the leadership of AESA Team Leadership. Lots of what Michael had been saying was fulfilled. Ebe had a fruitful ministry, visiting about thirty countries around the world for AE (though not preaching in all of them). The only thing that did not materialize was becoming AESA Team Leader. The reason for that was that Ebe had to flee the country when his life was threatened by the white government.

Seminars

Seminars worked well when they were held for a number of days in the city. These were very profitable. They were very difficult sometimes because the issues of apartheid were faced squarely. Issues were dealt with biblically as Christians prayed together, and sometimes cried together. It may have been true to say that most of the whites who attended believed that apartheid was wrong, but these meetings served to strengthen them, and their courage demonstrated to blacks that there were whites who honestly disagreed with the government's policy of oppression.

Ebenezer's first photo at age 15 in Weenen, KwaZulu-Natal, South Africa in 1946.

Ebenezer and Emily at their engagement party at the church-school where they taught near Stanger, South Africa in 1954.

On their wedding day near Stanger, on June 2, 1954.

Staff of Union Bible Institute where Ebenezer lectured for eleven years, in Sweetwaters, near Pietermaritzburg, 1968.

The African Enterprise team of Chris Smith, Abiel Thipanyane, Michael Cassidy, Ebenezer Sikakane and John Tooke at Mission '70 in Johannesburg, 1970.

Ebenezer and Emily with their five children in Pietermaritzburg while serving with African Enterprise, 1973.

With Dr. Billy Graham at a press conference in
Durban, South Africa, 1973.

Ebenezer and Emily with their children, spouses
and grandchildren in 2005.

X
UNIVERSITIES

The University of Zululand was also known as Ongoye. It was created by the white government under their policy of Separate Development and was exclusively black. The staff was mainly white, though there were also some black faculty members. AE was invited to hold an evangelistic mission on campus. Preparations went really well until the team actually got to the university. The white gentleman who was keen to have them come for the mission sounded very evangelical. He talked freely about the evils of radical students and assumed that AE, as evangelicals, were on the same page with him. As they were setting up the mission, they met some students who were very keen, and belonged to a good Christian group on campus. Some, however, were expecting the opposite. When AE finally converged on the campus, they discovered that whites wanted them there to convert the black radicals on campus. Black students, non-evangelicals, wanted them to come on campus and straighten out these white racists. Meetings were attended by people who had different agendas. All that was needed was for the AE preacher to open his/her mouth, and the audience knew whose side he/she was on. One had to walk a very tight rope in order not to lose the opportunity of reconciling the two. The Lord prevented a possible explosion. The situation was very polarized, and that is exactly where reconciliation was needed. It was indeed a cause for gratitude to the Lord that some students came to Christ under those circumstances. The Gospel is truly the power of God to save those who believe.

University of South Africa

This is not about a mission held at this university, but rather another saga—or twist and turn—of the story of apartheid. UNISA was a prestigious non-residential university. Ebe enrolled as a student for his bachelor's degree. Black students were not allowed to get into classrooms used by white students, so professors drove to the nearest black township to give lectures to black students in the months of June and July, when black schools were not in session. Ebe spent his winter vacations going to Atteridgeville Township outside Pretoria to attend these lectures held in a local high school. A Christian couple opened their home for him to stay with them for a couple of weeks while the lectures were going on. The husband was a deacon in a local Baptist church. His wife worked for a white man in Pretoria. She told Ebe stories, and he observed how she had to leave the house very early in the morning to get to work. He didn't hear her leave the house in the morning. She did this because she had to walk from her home to the train station, then walk again from the Pretoria Station to the employer's home to give him his first cup of coffee. Buses to the white suburb were for "Whites Only!" She returned very late, almost at night, everyday. She would occasionally be late for making the boss' first cup of coffee. In that case, she would phone her boss, who lived alone, and wake him up! She did this without spending five cents to make the call. The old South Africa public phones were easy to operate. You just lifted the receiver, cranked the little box, and it would start ringing. As soon as the operator picked it up on the other end, you would then drop the coin. Instead of dropping the coin, she would hang up, because she was sure he was awakened by the telephone ring and he was going to check the time.

Going back to Ebe's studies, he made this trip for several years. He spent several years working on his theology degree through UNISA, because it was a very tough university. They required a very high standard of work and he had a very heavy teaching schedule at UBI. However, he was able to fulfill all the requirements and in time became ready to graduate.

Ebe drove the family to Pretoria for his graduation. Emily had to be there for that. That was a great milestone for both of them. The ceremony was held under a large tent pitched on some dusty open ground in Atteridgeville. Blacks were not allowed to enter the University Hall even to graduate! They could not use facilities reserved for "Whites Only." You saw this sign everywhere in South Africa.

There was a smaller, adjoining tent that was to be used for refreshments after the ceremony. White ladies had been brought in to set this up for students to mix with their professors and families. But just as the ceremony was drawing to a close, there was a big rainstorm—thunder and lightning. It was beginning to drench all the white tablecloths and cookies. There was near-pandemonium as people tried to save the situation. Ebe was not sure how that ended. He simply got his family into the car and they left for home. That anti-climax simply ruined their day very sadly.

Examples of Unprovoked Brutality

Apartheid was brutal to blacks. Some whites enforced it with absolute cruelty, while other whites were very obviously opposed to it. It was usually those on the lower end in white society who were most threatened by blacks who seemed to be educated. These people's positions would be first to go to blacks. Ebe recalled taking his pretty new small car to a garage at a small town. The mechanic took one look at him and at the car he was driving and became inexplicably hostile. He took it out on his black "spanela boy" (or "spanner boy," a Zuluized English word). A spanner boy was a black man who was a "toolbox carrier" for a white box. Generally, a black man was derogatively addressed as "boy" regardless of age—even by a three-year-old child. The poor man looked stupefied by insults suddenly hurled at him by his boss for no reason.

Secondly, he remembered parking his motorcycle outside the home of a white man who was giving him some voice training in Scottsville in order for him to train the choir. Two white boys must have wondered what this black man was doing in the white suburb, so they cycled across the street and came straight to him. The one nearest to him rounded a whole lot of sputum in his mouth and spat on him, but just missed him. The sputum rested on the motorcycle saddle. Before reacting, he thought, *What would Jesus do?* That question quickly changed to, *Actually, what did Jesus do?* Jesus was spat upon! That settled it.

A full record of these instances would literally become boring after a while. South African blacks are truly and eternally thankful to the Lord for the change that has taken place in this beautiful country. The Sikakane family has been back to South Africa a number of times. They have seen and experienced what they never expected to see in their lifetime. The government seemed so intransigent, the police and the army seemed so invincible, that change in the system felt like an obvious impossibility. It certainly took a miracle of grace from above to bring about the change that we now see in South Africa.[2]

University of the North, 1975

The University of the North was also known as Turfloop, and it was another one of those universities created for blacks. It was in the province known then as the Northern Transvaal. It was supposed to cater for young people from the linguistic part of that province. However, they were economically forced to admit black students from other provinces. Our son, Ben, was admitted to that university.

---

[2] Read Michael Cassidy's book, entitled *A Witness For Ever*, regarding this miracle as was witnessed to by the world's secular press in 1994 in a matter of days before the expected blood bath took place.

When the political heat was accelerating in South Africa, AE's stand on reconciliation began to attract more and more students. Universities were beginning to call on AE to speak at their campuses. Organizations like the Student Christian Movement (SCM) were seriously grappling with political and ideological issues.

Their leaders were caught up in unenviable dilemmas. Marxism, Black Theology, and Liberation Theology were made attractive by their proponents.

An invitation came from the leader of the SCM at Turfloop for Ebe to team up with Bishop David Gitare from Nairobi, Kenya. They were both preaching and meeting with students. The meetings were not only public meetings for the proclamation of the Gospel—there was a lot of informal interaction with students seeking to understand and clarify the issues that Christian students were hit with left, right, and centre. They were dependent on the Holy Spirit to clarify these issues to them. Some students were radicalized with lots of misconceptions, yet believed that this was the direction from which solutions could possibly come. All that these missioners could do was bring forth some genuine indicators showing that the Gospel does have solutions that would ultimately be for the good of the country, as opposed to violence. One thing that AE was clear on in the discussions was that they were as opposed to apartheid as students were. The difference was on how to get rid of it. Christian students were prepared to give a hearing to Michael Cassidy, who was making a mark on the whole country. Some of those who were becoming sceptical of AE's approach to the South Africa situation were beginning to wonder if AE's was a better approach. The visitors were very impressed with the excellent leadership given by Frank, the SCM president, and his executive. He seemed very levelheaded and totally rejected the Bantustan policy.

University of Natal

The University of Natal was an all-white university during the days of apartheid. It was where Michael Cassidy spoke to professors, students, and ministers way back before the Mission to Maritzburg in 1961. This university was predisposed to AE even then. The Student Christian Association (SCA) of the university had a strong chapter there. Students were actively sharing the Christian message on campus.

The SCA invited Ebe to give his testimony at the campus. Students advertised the occasion widely on campus. When he arrived, Ebe was surprised to find a large number of students gathering at the lecture hall. The reason might have been because it was not common to have a black speaker. The atmosphere was very politically charged in those years. It was one of the universities where students were outspoken against apartheid while they were still studying. It became apparent to some blacks that once these students graduated, and faced issues of their bread and butter, the fight would be over. That was partly the reason that the Nationalist government increased their majority each general election.

Be that as it may, the majority of students in that group expected an explosive political speech. But Ebe's assignment was to give his testimony. After being introduced, he did just that. As soon as he mentioned the words, "I was converted," a white student sitting on the upper level of the lecture hall jumped on his feet and interrupted the meeting. He said something like this: "Your people are oppressed by white Christians. You have education. You ought to be working to liberate your people from their oppression. But instead you have been converted and become a white man!" Ebe responded by saying that their definitions of "Christian" were obviously different. He would never call his oppressors "Christians"—but before he concluded his sentence, the student shot back, "The whole cabinet is Christian. They go to church every Sunday. They don't read a newspaper on a Sunday. Isn't that Christian?" He stormed out of the meeting with his girlfriend. Ebe was going to explain that unlike other "religions" like Buddhism, Hinduism, Islam, and Judaism, Christianity is a personal relationship with Jesus Christ. Saul of Tarsus' religion was Judaism. He became a Christian after his relationship with Jesus Christ, by his conversion.

As a matter of fact, the meeting went on and went well, with the students' questions generating a good discussion after my testimony.

Botswana-Lesotho-Swaziland University (BLSU)

The AE team conducted an abbreviated mission to the University of BLS, which was held at Maseru, the capital of Lesotho. Even though it was held for several days, it was nonetheless a very strategic mission. Both the student body and faculty were different from the missions held in South Africa. Blacks in these three former British protectorates were very free politically and understood the plight of South African blacks who were still under apartheid. Students received the message well, because it met their need as Christian leaders in these democratic states. Students in BLSU were struggling with their own issues of poverty in their country, but these were different from the apartheid issues in South Africa.

Map of South Africa taken from African Enterprise book, *African Harvest.* Used with permission.

XI
CENTRAL AMERICA MISSIONS

Nicaragua

Some Central America evangelical leaders, whom AE had met during the Lausanne Congress on Mission and Evangelism in 1974, had expressed their desire to Michael Cassidy about having AE conduct an evangelistic mission in their part of the world. When the time was right, some team members went south, led by Michael Cassidy and Festo Kivengere, to another city in Nicaragua. Michael and Ebe flew together from New York to Nicaragua, and from there to Costa Rica. Before leaving, Professor Costas, the gentleman who had invited them to go to Central America, met with them for breakfast at a stopover in a hotel in New York where they had spent the night. He then drove them to JFK International Airport. Just as they drove up to the airport, he was talking away, not concentrating on where he was going. In the middle of orienting them to the culture and religious situation in Central America, he suddenly came to a fork in the road. Not knowing whether he should take the right or the left, he chose to take both roads! He banged the car onto the curb, reversed, and drove straight to the departures without stopping to check the damage! He only stopped to investigate when he got them out of the car. He discovered that the oil was leaking. He got into the car and sped away to find some help somewhere. His two passengers stepped out of his car and stood in disbelief, laughing their hearts out. Michael looked at Ebe and said, "This is our introduction to Central American driving."

That was very true. In Managua, the capital city, they took a taxi to visit a new Interdenominational Centre for Evangelicals. They nearly had three serious car accidents in that single trip. One example was coming to a traffic circle where it seemed as if all the several drivers had the right of way! No one seemed to know who had the right of way.

The crowning experience was their flight from Managua, Festo going to Blue Fields and Michael and Ebe to Puerto Cabesas where the meetings were to be held. By this time, they had met up and flew together with Bishop Festo Kivengere. Festo's party was going to be the first to deplane, whereas Michael and Ebe were heading for their destination. They took off in an old DC3. Halfway through the flight, Festo, who was sitting next to Ebe, said, "It looks as if we are heading back to Managua—you see which side the sun is on now." Sure enough, as they prepared to land, the runway was surrounded by several fire trucks. That was scary, to say the least. Only after landing did the pilot announce that he had to return because the plane had developed serious engine trouble.

Everybody moved to the airport building while a work crew moved in very leisurely, pulled out seats from the disabled passenger plane, and transferred them to an old cargo plane. It was so old that someone actually saw a rat in that cargo plane. It did not look much like an operative plane at all. Some were getting agitated by the delay. There was concern that if they delayed the moving of seats, the plane would run into a heavy afternoon rain, because the country was in a rainy season. That was the most frightening flight Ebe had ever experienced. There were no flying instruments. They flew it by sight. It was raining cats and dogs. Visibility was drastically reduced. Pilots had to keep their planes under thick dark clouds in order to see where they were going. Ebe said he sighed with relief as they landed at an old landing strip built by Americans during the last world war—or so someone had told them. If so, it had hardly been cared for since.

They dropped Festo's team at this landing strip and that is where Ebe was convinced the pilot was not so irresponsible to venture beyond considering those terrifying conditions. Indeed, he had written a note for Emily, wrapped it in plastic, and placed it in his briefcase—bidding her farewell, just in case! He heard two things that consoled him somewhat. First, when he expressed his concern, Michael's response was that these pilots had their own lives to protect and would not place themselves in danger. Secondly, one of those who had come to meet their friends, who were all also taking shelter from the pouring rain by standing under the wings of the plane, said,

"Oh, they have this pilot. He is the best." That was the best thing he had heard all day. From that point on, the plane flew over the ocean, flying quite low because there was probably no danger of hitting a mountain that way. They landed safely in Puerto Cabesas and breathed a big sigh of relief.

Meetings were held in a very large hall belonging to the Roman Catholic church. They estimated that it could seat nearly two thousand people. It was pretty full over the weekend. Michael did most of the preaching. Ebe did some, too. One morning, they were interviewed live by the local radio station. One important assignment they received was going out to preach in a prison which had notorious criminals. After preaching what seemed to me like a very anointed message, Michael made an appeal. Probably the most notorious prisoner came forward, with a good number of others, and they all gave their lives to Christ. He had made a pact with Satan that he was going to kill all his siblings plus his parents. He had already killed some of his family. The translator was a powerful Spanish-speaking evangelist, Roberto Barrientos. He was small in stature, but roared like a lion when he spoke with his big and forceful voice.

The gentleman who was emcee and introduced the speakers at each meeting had memorized Ebe's last name incorrectly. After introducing him a few times, he asked if he had pronounced it correctly. Ebe then felt free to correct him as to how "Sikakane" was to be spoken. The next time he introduced him, he messed it up again. As he struggled with it, someone shouted from the audience to just call him "Sugarcane"! The confusion was further complicated by Bishop Festo

Kivengere, who was on the list of evangelists to Nicaragua. So, Ebe ended up being called "Bishop Sugarcane" and, of course, Festo was called Bishop Kilimanjaro! Michael had quite a time describing his colleagues, who were as high as Mount Kilimanjaro and as sweet as Sugarcane.

They saw incredible contrasts in the small town. They stayed in a posh hotel nestled in abject poverty surroundings. The rich and the poor were poles apart. The menu at the hotel had a long list of choices—some of the items looked like exotic and rare stuff. Michael suggested one evening that he would ask about some of these items just to see if they were really available. And they were! The team heard that Dictator Somosa would drink, dine, and dance there with his cohorts from time to time.

The team took a walk around the neighbourhood one morning and noticed a pathetic situation. They gained a better understanding of why Liberation Theology had flourished in that part of the continent. There was a gaping chasm between the rich and the poor. The wattle and daub houses were in very bad shape. Each of them had an elevated floor resting on strong poles which were several feet apart. That provided shelter for the family's animals, like goats, pigs, and whatever else the family owned. Another reason for placing the floor on some elevated foundation was to keep the floor as dry as possible during the rainy season.

WRESTLING WITH APARTHEID

Costa Rica

From Nicaragua, part of the AE team moved on to Costa Rica where they worked closely with American missionaries who understood Central America well. The team spent fewer days in a town called Puerto Limon. The city seemed depressed and showed no sign of any well-off people. There was fierce competition between pastors, bordering on jealousy. Another striking thing was the number of liquor stores! That revealed a lot about the town, which might have been a fair symptom of the problem that the town of Limon faced. Nearly every couple of blocks was a liquor store. It seemed utterly out of proportion to everything else you saw in that town. Yet on the other hand, the school that Ebe visited and spoke in was a good school. That primary school had a very good principal. Her pupils asked some outstanding questions on apartheid. They were the most perceptive students he had met anywhere in understanding the problems of South Africa.

XII
INTERNATIONAL CONGRESSES

There were four congresses on evangelism that Ebe participated in. These congresses provided great opportunities of growth, challenge, and encouragement to the church worldwide. They had a real potential to enable it to play its role of being a reconciling force in the world. Africa was terribly fragmented politically, economically, religiously, socially, and otherwise. Festo Kivengere once passionately described Africa as the "bleeding continent." But it also held the great potential of being the fulcrum in world mission and evangelism. African and Asian representation in these world congresses was significant. They encouraged the church in developing countries to play their role in world evangelism. Africa had to be part of the solution rather than part of the problem. This was AE's vision. No one could ever pretend to be able to solve the complex problems of Africa. But seeing them in these congresses was a ray of hope.

WRESTLING WITH APARTHEID

The Durban Congress, 1973

There was no end to the hurdles that had to be crossed before the Durban Congress became a reality. The best and most well-known evangelical world leaders converged on the South African soil when apartheid was at the pinnacle of its power. For the first time, it seemed as if apartheid had been waived. Black and white lived together in a hotel, traveled and sang together on buses that were normally segregated, ate together in dining rooms that were for "Whites Only," and swam together in the white swimming pool of the hotel, thus blowing away the minds of the watching black employees of the hotel. A wide range of papers were presented, seminars and workshops held, all dealing with the role of the church within apartheid South Africa and the African continent. South African leaders got to meet some of the very most well-known Christian leaders from around the world.

Billy Graham was the main attraction of the world press gathered in Durban. South African churches had tried for twenty years to get him to come and hold a crusade in South Africa, but he would not come because they could not guarantee that he would preach to mixed audiences. Michael met Graham's condition, so he came. They asked Ebe to introduce and present him at the press conference held in one of the hotels. At the press conference, Graham was peppered with questions, mainly about apartheid. He answered them as wisely as only Graham could do. At the large rally held at the stadium in Durban, Ebe interpreted for him, facing the isiZulu speaking crowd gathered in one large section assigned to them. He had spent a whole afternoon with Billy in his hotel suite going through his message based on Saul's conversion (Acts 9). Ebe realized what a humble servant of God Billy Graham was. They spent about three hours together and Graham wanted to get to know Ebe. He indeed got to know him to the best of his ability before he interpreted for him. Graham's message was typed in very large print. When they met in Amsterdam some ten years later, and Ebe introduced himself, reminding him that he was his interpreter in Durban, Billy said, "Oh yes, your picture is on the wall with others in our dining room."

The Lausanne, Switzerland Congress, 1974

Thousands of evangelists from every corner of the world attended the Lausanne, Switzerland Congress. It was sponsored by the Billy Graham Association. There was a large contingent of black and white delegates from South Africa. The congress worked hard under the leadership of Dr. John Stott, producing the well-known document called the Lausanne Covenant. All the delegates had input in the formation of this document. There were sessions in which delegates were divided into national groups to come up with a strategy for evangelizing their nations. When it came to the South Africa group, the meetings were explosive. Blacks felt it was hypocritical for them to pretend that whites and blacks could unite just because they were outside the country and pretend to plan something that they knew would never be practical in their divided country. This was probably not as explosive as the Berlin Congress of 1966, however, where some white ministers from South Africa demanded that Michael Cassidy's paper be expunged from the Congress compendium because it came down too hard on apartheid.

In Lausanne, black delegates were looking for some agreement between themselves as Christians to work together to challenge apartheid. They felt that white evangelicals were trying to put on a façade to mislead the world regarding the true conditions in South Africa. Some of those evangelicals were honest people attempting to do something they would never do in South Africa for fear of being ostracized. Blacks were amazed to find that upon arrival in Lausanne, blacks from South Africa had been allocated an all-black accommodation which seemed to be in perpetuation of the South Africa policy. Anyway, some whites noticed this and voluntarily "crossed the floor" and came to share accommodation with blacks. This provided a good opportunity for them to interact with each other, share facilities like bathrooms, etc.

There were plenary sessions in the evenings when they had superb speakers, usually two. One evening that stood out in Ebe's mind was when Professor Muggeridge (the British intellectual) teamed up with Dr. E.V. Hill (an African American from Los Angeles). It was an exciting clash of cultures, indeed. Hill's illustrations were heavily based on baseball—America's popular game. He talked about "first base, third base, home run." Many delegates had no inklings of what that was all about. When he returned to the Bible, he had delegates eating from the palm of his hand.

INTERNATIONAL CONGRESSES

A Visit to Israel

From Lausanne, Ebe took a short hike to Israel, which was a wonderful experience for him. He had finalized arrangements in Lausanne with Victor Smadja, a great Israeli Christian leader. He flew to Israel via Rome. As they were about to land in Rome, an Indian gentleman came and sat next to Ebe. The plane was not full. After exchanging a few words about Rome and hearing that Ebe was going to get a taxi to his hotel, he warned him about taxi drivers who would charge you the after midnight fare by pressing the meter twice. His driver did exactly what the passenger had said. Ebe motioned him pointing at his watch speaking in English. He pretended he did not understand what Ebe was saying with all his gestures. As he tried to ignore him, Ebe opened the door and pretended to jump out of his moving taxi. In disbelief, he stopped the taxi and changed the meter. Upon arrival at the hotel, Ebe left his luggage being unloaded and asked the receptionist to come out and check the meter and to pay him the correct amount.

He spent a few days in Rome and visited the Vatican. Pope John XXIII passed few yards in front of him aboard his open coupe. He had lots of interesting experiences in Rome. The day he flew out to Israel, security at the Rome airport was so thorough that a lady who carried a pineapple had it cut in half to ensure that there was nothing in it. When he arrived at the airport in Tel Aviv, Victor was not there to meet him, as prearranged. He could not find his name in the phone book, because he was unlisted. Victor was in the printing business in Jerusalem, publishing books proving that Jesus was the Messiah. They later met and he took Ebe to the guest house within the walls of Jerusalem. He and some other tourists had an "illegal" Palestinian guide who was a Christian and drove them to all the places they wanted to see. He provided enough Bibles for his passengers and quoted chapter and verse from stories connected with places they visited. He would not enter certain places where only official Jewish guides were allowed.

One unforgettable experience was when the guide dropped Ebe near the Empty Tomb. Entering the empty tomb was an overwhelmingly emotional experience. Just getting in there and pausing to pray, and imagining that it was there that Christ was laid, that it was there where He arose to now live at the right hand of His Father, was a very emotional time for him and for all who were there. He could not remain too long in there, because other tourists needed to enter. So they went out and sat on provided park benches and chairs for meditation. One white lady who was totally overcome by emotions staggered over and sat next to Ebe, just weeping, and she threw her arm over his shoulder and they prayed together. They never talked. She joined her group and they vanished.

The other experience, second only to the Empty Tomb experience, was when Victor called and told him that the visiting speaker he was expecting to have at his church was unable to enter the country. So instead he was asking Ebe to speak the next day, Saturday morning. That was humbling. To think, he was having to speak at the chosen people's time of worship! It was going to be an unrepeatable experience for him. He could hardly sleep that Friday night. Their time together was wonderful. The congregation was composed of younger families who were alive spiritually. The singing was fantastic.

The Zimbabwean Congress, 1976

The Zimbabwean Congress was tackled by a smaller team consisting of Michael Cassidy, John Tooke, and Ebe, who flew up to Bulawayo in Rhodesia to attend. Guerilla warfare in the region was hot at that point and the idea was that the local black and white clergy had to own the Congress. Christians were deeply divided and they needed to be bridge-builders and catalysts for change. They had to read papers that were relevant to their situation as they understood it. They had to propose biblical solutions that would enable them to build bridges across colour lines. The team was there in a supportive role. Tensions were running very high, but there were some great Christian leaders on both sides of the divide. On a Sunday, Ebe was scheduled to speak at a church in Bulawayo. He lined up a translator. They arrived at the church in good time. They waited outside as people came in. Ebe noticed an elderly lady carrying what looked very much like a Zulu Bible. He asked if he could look at her Bible. She gave it to him. He exclaimed, "You use the isiZulu Bible here! Can you really understand it? This is my language!" She thought Ebe was crazy to be so excited about something that was normal. Anyway, he abandoned his interpreter and preached in isiZulu and the Ndebeles could understand him. When he shared this experience with the team, he did not realize that he was going to end up interpreting for Dr. Ralph Bell, the black team member of the

Billy Graham Association. Ralph was to preach at a large rally held at the Bulawayo Stadium.

The Nairobi Congress, 1976

The Nairobi Congress was held in December 1976 in Kenya. The AE team was in free Africa, and so the Congress was to deal with a different set of problems. Therefore, the congress was structured differently. In fact, it was called the Pan-African Christian Leadership Assembly (PACLA). The whole aim of the assembly was to gather the younger Christian leaders of Africa together, from the university level up, to examine ways and means of establishing the Church biblically in the African continent. This was not easy, because in some parts of Africa young people could not really provide leadership to the church. AE went ahead and invited young leaders anyway. Some mature leaders showed up, which was fine as long as they were accompanied by prospective younger leaders. The continent's Christianity was, and still is, described as a mile long and a quarter of an inch deep. Moreover the continent had the largest population of independent churches which hardly had a clue of what the Gospel was all about.

In fact, prior to PACLA, Ebe had had a long interview with Dr. David Barrett on the subject of the independent churches in South Africa. This was before Dr. Barrett produced his comprehensive Encyclopedia on World Missions. It was during that stay in Kenya that Ebe was introduced to Professor Stephen Neill, who was at the time teaching at the university in Nairobi. He was one of the many people who were interested in understanding the situation of apartheid in South Africa. Ebe even saw himself on TV very briefly for the first time ever. A journalist from Madagascar had spoken to him in front of the cameras. That little footage was beamed from Madagascar. There was no TV in South Africa at that time. The apartheid government did not want blacks to have exposure to how people lived in the rest of the world!

The delegates to PACLA came from nearly every country on the continent, even from some Islamic countries. Their coming had to be kept hush-hush. The Jomo Kenyatta Convention Centre was used for the occasion. The highest officials of Kenya were very helpful to AE, trying to get white delegates from South Africa to enter the country. Kenya, as well as most other African countries, had no diplomatic relations with South Africa. The few exceptions were Malawi, under Kamuzu Banda, and Cote d'Ivoire, under President Felix Houphouet-Boigny, which still retained diplomatic relationships with the white regime in South Africa. It was to the shame and disappointment of the AE team when later they wanted to reciprocate that good gesture by Kenyans. They invited some Christian dignitaries from Kenya to visit Pietermaritzburg, South Africa. They were allowed into the country but were refused service in a restaurant. They were deeply humiliated when they were taken out of the restaurant despite efforts by John Tooke urging the manager not to further alienate South Africa. The Nairobi Congress had done a lot to link South Africa with the rest of the continent. This cruel act in a restaurant was very embarrassing.

Incidentally, Kenya was the first African country that Ebe visited. He went to Nairobi in 1972. He attended a writers' conference that convened in Limuru, outside Nairobi. It was to encourage and train young African authors. He had written a number of booklets in isiZulu, and so he was invited to attend. This conference was probably sponsored by Tyndale House Publishers in Wheaton, because Dr. Ken Taylor, the author of the Living Bible series, was there. In fact, Ebe was privileged to be in the discussion group led by Dr. Taylor. He was later encouraged to join up with Bernard Johanson, and translate Dr. Taylor's series into isiZulu. But as the would-be translators discussed the project, they did not see the need of it. They had to convince missionaries who were ready to embark on fundraising for that translation. The Bible in isiZulu was not in a King James Version (KJV) type of language. Younger people spoke isiZulu as it was written in the Bible. Therefore, there was no need for the Living Translation in isiZulu.

Singapore to Hong Kong

Most of the AE team joined in with a number of organizations that attended a conference in Singapore. Ebe was on the team to Singapore in 1978. They were on what he called a chartered plane which was to leave from Nairobi and fly as far as Hong Kong. The ticket would only be cheaper if the whole group flew beyond Singapore! Their first stop was in Sri Lanka. It was fascinating to visit the capital city, Colombo. There was so much to see there around the city. People went to visit different areas of the city—to see ivories and tiger teeth turned into beautiful costly jewellery and some other ivory products. Other people even went on elephant rides! Time limitations made it impossible to stay long in the city. There were some strong Christians from Sri Lanka that Ebe had met in Switzerland at the Lausanne Congress. It was not possible to meet with them in Colombo.

From Sri Lanka, the group flew to Singapore This small republic off the southern tip of the Malay peninsula, was a member of the British Commonwealth in 1965. Most of the people spoke English, which was the main language. There were some highly educated speakers at the conference. In one of the sessions just before the time of worship, a lady chatted with Ebe for a while, and then shocked him when she asked if she could touch and feel his hair! He was so embarrassed that, if he were not umZulu, he would have blushed. But Zulu blood is not close to the surface of the skin, so his face did not turn red. Another surprise came when he was walking on the overpass. A gentleman going in the opposite direction walked straight towards him, gazing at him all the time, even stopping and turning his head as he passed. He gave the impression that he had not seen someone black at such a close range. Delegates visited different churches on the Sunday they were there. They experienced good worship and great preaching.

The group moved on to Hong Kong. They stayed in a good hotel, which was part of their airfare package. They spent about two nights. The following morning, ground transportation took them to a handful of chosen stores to do their shopping. Among the stores were jewellery shops or men's/

women's clothing stores, where you would choose cloth, get measured, and pick it up the next morning! Those who had that kind of money had their suits cut and sewn to perfection by the following day. When you see that kind of business genius, you realize how people make their money.

Some of the places they were shown were schools where children were taught on the roofs of high rises, because there was not enough land to build schools. Lots of the churches met in large hotel rooms on Sundays. They told the group that one had to obtain permission to purchase a car after proving that one had a garage for it. Someone drove them to the border of Hong Kong and China. The big road was tarred on the Hong Kong side, leading up to a locked gate. On the Chinese side, it was simply two parallel wheel trails with grass between the wheel tracks.

XIII

MOVE TO
CANADA (1978)

The Sikakane family chose to move to Canada because, as already indicated, Reverend Ken Wardle and his wife Hazel had promised to assist them in finding a United Church to sponsor them. Indeed, the United Church of Canada (UCC) had lots of openings.

It had become very evident that someday Ebe was going to be called in for interrogation regarding his movements in and out of South Africa. Being called for interrogation was a frightening thing, because such people could be detained for up to 380 days without trial. So when their papers were ready for Canada, Ebe and Emily fled the country with their five children. They moved at different times. Their son Ebenson and daughter Rosemary moved first to join their parents who were at Fuller Seminary at the time. They were ready to start going to college. Ebenson attended George Fox College in Oregon. Rosemary joined Dr. and Mrs. Schut's family in Minnesota to start school at Bethel College. Primrose moved to Pennsylvania alone to join the Betty and Mel Swanson family, who had found her a high school called Pinebrook near their home. Later, the twins, Crown and Wiseman, followed their siblings to the United States. They went to Nassell High School in Washington State.

Three Churches in Quebec

Ebe and Emily were the last to leave their home. That was one of the most difficult decisions they had ever made. Imagine pulling the door shut behind you, turning your back on your beautiful home, your extended family, your country, your ministry, and your friends. They had to leave behind the cherished surroundings on Dambuza Road, in Edendale just outside Pietermaritzburg. It was hard even to sell some of their stuff, like a pretty new car they owned, the Peugeot 404.

The United Church of Canada had accepted Ebe's application and credentials for a job and paid for all their passage expenses to Canada. They gave him three churches to pastor (a three-point charge). One was Sept-Iles (Seven-Islands), where they were based, located about 350 miles north of Quebec City. But the farthest of the three churches was Schefferville, a further three or four hundred miles north of Sept-Iles. This town was not accessible by road. There was a train that took forever to get there. So Ebe flew free of charge periodically to Gagnon and Schefferville in the local iron ore company plane. He was given free hotel accommodation in Gagnon, and stayed with an Anglican couple in Schefferville who were co-priests of the Anglican Church there.

The Sept-Iles congregation was like a community church. It was one of two English-speaking Protestant churches with a collection of people from different churches—Salvation Army, Baptists, Presbyterians, etc. Members were by and large upper-middle class whites who were mainly in managerial positions in the iron ore industry. Iron ore was the main source of income for the whole city. The overwhelming majority of the city's residents were French speaking. The single French family that Ebe led to Christ came reluctantly to worship with English-speaking people. He and his family came in through the front door and went out the back door—for good! They felt like fish out of water. They were extremely uncomfortable in the midst of all the English-speaking people. Ebe was a reconciler, encouraging them to attend so that they might begin to relate and learn some English. They obviously had no intention of learning it. They did not need it! Ebe ended up recommending that they join a French Pentecostal church. The good bilingual pastor there was a friend of Ebe's, who preached in his church when Ebe was away.

Quebec was very tense the year the Sikakanes arrived. It was just prior to the Referendum. Premier Levesque wanted Quebec to break away from Canada and become an independent country. On one hand, the French were "smelling" the day of their independent Quebec; on the other hand, English-speaking members of Ebe's church were very scared, to say the least, because the polls were indicating that Premier Levesque was going to win the Referendum. The English were concerned about what was going to happen to them. Some came to the pastor and wondered what they could do to improve relationships with their neighbours. It was somewhat of a surprise to people from the land torn apart by apartheid to find that the tensions in the province were almost as strong as those in South Africa. There was at least some interracial dialogue in South Africa, however limited. Christians were talking to and praying with each other, but not in Sept-Iles.

In Sept-Iles, life was good but very challenging. Pastoring an all-white church was very strange, coming out of South Africa. Some of those well-to-do whites had never really been close to blacks. Local people expected them to speak French, because the only black people they saw on TV were French-speaking blacks from West Africa. The experience Ebe and Emily had working with African Enterprise came in handy. They could relate comfortably with members of the congregation. The top leadership of the denomination accepted them well. They even more than tolerated his evangelical stance. They asked Ebe twice to lead Bible studies at their Presbytery gatherings, with the moderator present.

The Language Problem

French posed a real problem for the Sikakanes, and especially their children. Primrose entered a college in Quebec City. Crown and Wiseman entered the Queen Elizabeth High School (a misnomer, since this English-named school taught so predominantly in French) in Sept-Iles. They could not enter university after just one year of high school. They were not even studying French. The notorious Bill 101 (enforcing exclusive use of French in Quebec) precluded that. The "Cegep" (pre-university year) in the province of Quebec was taught in French only. So the family had to move out of Quebec after serving for eighteen months in order to find a church in any English-speaking province of Canada. They thought that it would be easy to find one, but that was a gross underestimation of the problem. They drew blanks from many United Church congregations they contacted.

Move to Toronto, 1980

After trying and failing to find a church in any English-speaking province of Canada, Ebe found that it was even harder to break into the city of Toronto, because every minister in the denomination wanted a church in the city, for obvious reasons. A number of churches turned him down after interviewing him or after seeing his resume. Coming to another one of the interviews in Toronto, he spent a night with Bill and Gina Lamb. This couple knew Michael Cassidy, and supported African Enterprise. When he mentioned to them that he had taught at a Bible School in South Africa, and sensing his frustration, Gina asked if he had applied to OBC. "What is that?" he asked. She said it was the Ontario Bible College. After getting back to Sept-Iles, he submitted his application for a teaching position to this unknown Ontario Bible College. Gina was one of the referrals. She sat on the board of the Corporation of the college.

There was no response for weeks. All of a sudden, a phone call came from the academic dean, Dr. Bob Duez. He told him that the Chairman of the Missions Department was retiring, and that his resume with his degree from Fuller's School of World Mission qualified him for the position. He flew down to Toronto for two interviews. The next morning, he was to face the entire faculty and be interviewed by them. He was petrified. He could not imagine the daunting task he would be facing the following day. He woke up early and had his devotions, walking around the whole campus seven times. Even though he did not blow any trumpet after each round, he trusted that the imaginary walls of Jericho would come crashing down and allow him in. They did! And he was to spend the next sixteen years with OBC, which later became Tyndale University College and Seminary.

He had to learn the ropes in a hurry, because he had no idea what the head of a department was supposed to do. Bob was extremely helpful. He patiently walked him through the whole process. Dr. Victor Adrian, the president, was equally helpful and accepted him gracefully, and seemed to have confidence that he would be able to do just fine. The college president simply had genuine love for Africa. He knew a number of Africans, some of whom Ebe did not know. So, before long, Ebe settled down to teaching and administering the department.

President Dr. Vic Adrian from Winnipeg, and the late academic dean Dr. Bob Duez, showed great leadership in seeing that which Ebe did not see in himself—a man whom a white boy in South Africa had spat upon—and trusting him with the position of the head of the Department of Missions. Ebe, spending sixteen years of teaching in that position, until his retirement, spoke volumes of their faith in him. Later on, when Ebe was retiring, he recommended a very gifted student to be his successor. Due to the fact that the status of the college, specifically the Intercultural Studies Department, was changing, he could not succeed Ebe. The student is, however, doing a magnificent job as a Bible translator in Africa.

The OBC Classroom

The response from his classes was amazing. Remember, he was from South Africa. He had never sat with white students in a class until he got to Fuller Seminary. At OBC, his classes were overwhelmingly white. And many students passed through his "hands" each year because one of the courses he taught was a core course—required to be taken by every freshman. In his sixteen years of lecturing there, literally hundreds of students sat in his classes. No wonder ten years after his retirement he still met his former students at nearly every Christian gathering he attended in Ontario and beyond. And they still commented about his classes.

Ebe had a lot of fun with some students, as well as serious challenges. Ebe related one incident like this. "I once observed our class 'clown' giggling with the guy sitting next to him. He then raised his hand. I knew that something was afoot! The student said, 'Sir, a friend of mine asked me a question which I could not answer. He said to me, when were black people created? We find no record of this happening in Genesis.' I responded by saying, 'It's funny how people ask such funny questions. An acquaintance of mine once asked me a similar question, slightly different. He said to me, when did God create all these white people, who seem not to have been fully baked and have to go to Florida to get some suntan in order to complete their creation?' The class roared with laughter!"

Urbana Students Conference

There were a number of important things that Ebe did together with students, majoring in missions both on campus and off-campus. The popular Urbana Students Mission Conference in Illinois was one of those. He attended a number of Urbana conferences with OBC students. This took a lot of planning, but it was worth it. Some Canadian churches became very involved in this project by encouraging their students, and helping them with the needed funds. The international students were the ones who had no way of raising funds for it. A few individuals did support some international students. One such individual who was keen to assist international students to go to Urbana was Jack Gibson. He was prepared to assist almost as many African students as were able to attend. This gentleman, a businessman from High Park Baptist Church, was very missionary minded. He put his money where his mouth was.

There were lot of spiritual preparations that preceded the trip to Urbana, mainly because the organizers put a lot of effort into preparing things like small group Bible studies. Missionaries who had booths there were very helpful to the students. Top Bible teachers and Gospel preachers were a great blessing to thousands of students who attended Urbana.

Ebe spoke only once at Urbana, and it was not during the main conference. He spoke at the after-meeting of international students on January 1-4. The subject given to him to speak on was Theology of Missions. The students in attendance were a keen and enthusiastic group. And they were a mature group, too. They mainly came from Asia, and were studying in the United States. Their student leaders were equally enthusiastic about their ministry.

There was an interesting episode that occurred at one of the main Urbana conferences. Ebe met a group of students from South Africa! At a breakfast table, he sat with a couple of them. This was a big surprise for him. After introductions around the table, one daring American student who noticed how excited they were to meet each other inquired what blacks and whites were fighting about in South Africa, "when you guys are so friendly." Here they loved each other and were excited about what was happening in Urbana. One of the two missionary kids (MKs) piped up almost before the guy had completed the question and said, "We have no problem in South Africa. It's just troubles created by a few misguided individuals inspired by communists. And of course blacks can never govern South Africa. Different tribes would simply fight each other. Isn't it so, Mr. Sikakane?"

This was the sort of stuff white kids were fed at school, and possibly at home as well. After listening to Ebe's response, the student probably did not know how to swallow his words. Ebe did not know those young people. He knew their parents, because he had preached at their mission stations when they were at boarding school. They also recognized his name. They just assumed that as a good evangelical, Ebe would never see anything wrong done by the government. They were absolutely stunned by his response, because apparently they had never discussed politics with any black person in South Africa. They had imbibed everything they learned from racists in school.

Hands-On Experience

One of the objectives of the missions major in training students to be missionaries was to do so by taking them to some cross-cultural ministry situations that would serve as a hands-on experience for them. They had to take students to a totally different culture so they could learn to live, work, and interact with people there. They had to observe how other cultures lived, what they ate, how they dressed, how they perceived the world—their worldview. This meant more than just taking them to ethnic areas of Toronto, which they did. Groups of students would visit sections of the city which were predominantly, say, Chinese, Greek, Italian, Somali, or Jamaican. They would observe all they could, order and taste their food, and visit their churches.

Short-Term Mission to Jamaica, 1990

The first country the short-term mission team took on was Jamaica. It was not like visiting parts of Toronto where Jamaicans lived and traded, but they decided to go to Jamaica to build some homes that had been destroyed by a hurricane. They worked in conjunction with Emmanuel International, which was already committed to ministry in Jamaica. Preparations took a long time. Fundraising for airfares, expenses on the ground, and building material to be purchased once the team got there turned out to be a big job. Buying materials in the hosting country would help the country's economy. So, cash raised for that purpose was taken to Jamaica. They did some orientation before leaving Canada, and also when they got to Jamaica. Local leaders did some specific orientation on the ground. It was made plain to the students that their role was to assist and supply Jamaican builders with materials. They were not builders themselves. Jamaica had skilled builders that they would be helping. They were also going to help on Sundays as well, as requested.

There were three professors on the team from OBC, each one heading a building team—the late Dr. Bob Duez, and Dr. Henry Friesen. Each of the three teams completed a two-room house during the weeks they were there. The Jamaican builders were very competent and had drawn plans and ordered building materials before the arrival of the team from Canada. There were things that were unexpected, and contrary to the usual stereotypes held about developing countries. For instance, one of these stereotypes was blown away the very first Sunday they attended a church service. It is common knowledge in the west that people in Jamaica keep Jamaican time. Well, everybody was in church before the Canadians arrived! The Canadians were five minutes late. Jamaicans did not keep walking in halfway into worship, as is generally portrayed. Nearly all the Sunday school kids whom students had to teach were carrying a copy of the Bible and a Hymn Book. And they were clean and neatly dolled up! This blew the Canadians away.

One thing that irritated some of the students was a rooster that woke them up by crowing at about 4:00 a.m. A couple of the students were so aggravated that they went out and threw some objects up the big, generously-leafed tree where the rooster was crowing, even though they were warned not to do so. Otherwise the project went as planned. Teams were driven to and from work. They enjoyed themselves and they had plenty of good food and fruit. It proved to be a maturing experience for the students. They returned to Toronto encouraged. There were opportunities for them to report back to their supporting churches.

Short-Term Mission to Ghana, 1992

David Mensah was one of the outstanding students at OBC. After graduating, he started making comprehensive plans to return to his neglected Northern Ghana. He hoped to establish a strong Christian witness in that part of Ghana. And he planned to teach farming to widows who were destitute. Some of those women were abandoned by their husbands. David and his dear wife, Brenda, a Canadian, were planning to develop poor Northern Ghana as a whole. They are currently continuing to implement their plans, which are flourishing, and are realizing the fulfillment of their vision.

A short-term mission was planned after they had returned to Ghana from Canada. Ebe helped students raise support for the group planning to go there. They also found help given by CIDA (Canadian International Development Agency). There was additional logistical assistance given by the Christian Children's Fund organization. Among the assignments given to students was to help dig water wells, as well as other projects already in progress at a village called Janga.

The Canadians had a rousing welcome from the chief of the tribes in the Janga area. David had a good rapport with the now deceased Muslim chief. A big Canadian flag was flying on a huge tree in the centre of his palace. He personally met and welcomed them in their traditional way—lots of happiness and traditional dancing by literally hundreds of people who had gathered there. There was another warm welcome when the whole group from Canada paid a courtesy call to the Canadian embassy. They also visited a mission station with which David had a good relationship. While there, they were treated to a lovely dinner, but unfortunately all caught a stomach bug. It was probably not caused by food or water, because the local Ghanaians caught it, too.

The students helped complete four water wells to serve well-chosen communities interspersed in the tribal area. As a safety precaution, the Canadian government officials had prohibited the students from going down the water well for any reason. They could only bring building materials to the builders. David had acquired the services of a competent young man, trained in England, to get down the well and lay bricks efficiently. He did a good job. The students provided the needed unskilled labour. They mixed mortar and lowered that and the bricks down to the young man. Other students helped in completing the multi-roomed centre where they were accommodated, installing tanks to catch rainwater for use in the centre.

Ebe helped raise an amount of $11,000 (USD) for the work and upkeep expenses. David arranged with a bank to change all that money to cedis (the local currency). It translated into millions of cedis, which meant that David was carrying a couple of bulging bags full of cash when they walked out of the bank! Ghana's economy was not good at the time, even though the country looked much better than it had on Ebe's previous visit to Ghana. Shops had hardly anything on the shelves then, and the merchandise that was available cost too much money. But this time around, there was a marked improvement in the economy.

Before their return to Canada, Ebe had arranged to meet with Emily in Amsterdam. They were to fly to South Africa the next day. They spent that day looking around the city. It was easy to do that since when you get off the plane, and take an escalator downstairs to catch an underground train that takes you to the heart of the city. In the evening, they boarded a flight to Johannesburg. They spent ten days visiting Emily's family in Newcastle and Ebe's in Estcourt. They went around the rest of KwaZulu-Natal, seeing friends and former school colleagues. Needless to say, it was a refreshing time for them.

This was a good break for Emily, who had been working hard at the Mini Skool Daycare Center back home in Canada. As a room supervisor, she faced challenging times and decisions from time to time. She seemed to do more working than supervising. She learned many interesting lessons—some of them sad. The administration did not allow daycare kids to learn anything about religion. At lunch time, they were not allowed to use "religious jargon," like pray! The teachers had to say, "Let us say the words." A devoted Muslim lady used the break as an opportunity to take the Koran, kneel on a velvet mat, and pray, facing the east. The rest of the staff knew who the religious people were.

When a friend of Emily, originally from England, was diagnosed with terminal cancer, she began to grow closer to Emily. Before she passed away, she asked Emily if Ebe could conduct her funeral. Emily and Ebe went to her apartment to pray with her and make arrangements for the funeral. She seemed pretty ready to go and had dealt with a number of things. Those included remarrying her ex-husband and asking him to take care of their two sons, who had been her sole responsibility. She bravely got to prepare the program for her funeral after purchasing her own coffin.

Short-Term Mission to Colombia, 1994

Taking a team of students to this country was not easy. It was a challenging assignment, mainly because of negative reports in the media. Latin America Mission advised Ebe not to go to Bogota, but rather to Cartagena, a port city of Colombia on the Caribbean. There was not a lot of political activity and turmoil there, even though they could not really understand what was going on because only a few people spoke English.

Newspapers and television programs were all in Spanish. The Canadian team stayed with the family of a wonderful Christian, a dentist, who had become a pastor. The church he was planting met in his own house. There was hardly any privacy for his family, it seemed, because people came and went freely, and entered just about every room. Many cultures would feel as if that was an invasion of their freedom, but it did not seem to bother this wonderful couple.

There were a number of projects the Canadian team undertook in Cartagena. They repaired a couple of schools which were in bad shape. In another township, they turned the gable of a church roof, which had been inconveniencing the neighbours a great deal. Every time it rained, the water would pour into the yard of the neighbours. The gable had to be changed from facing north-south to facing east-west.

Students had more opportunities in Cartagena to go witnessing and work with translators in schools, and with late teens and university students who spoke some English. The students related very well to them. They had pizza gatherings with young people just as they did in Canada. Their behaviour was also pretty similar.

The flight back to Toronto from Cartagena was the five hundredth flight for Ebe, and one student whispered that to one flight attendant who arranged for him to take a peak at the cockpit. Apparently, this was a big deal.

MOVE TO CANADA

Seattle Pacific College, 1984

Before coming to OBC, Ebenezer had traveled to Seattle a number of times on behalf of African Enterprise. One of the places he had visited was the Seattle Pacific College. He had met the head of the Missions Program there, and developed a good relationship with him. When this man was on the point of retiring from SPC, his friends, who had been missionaries in South Africa, advised him to get in touch with an African professor of missions who was teaching at OBC in Canada to see if he might be interested in coming to SPC as his successor. They gave Ebe a good recommendation, because they had gotten to know Ebe well in South Africa. The retiring professor, Dr. Kline, had not known that Ebe was in Canada. So things seemed to come together as they had spoken often about these same missionaries when Ebe was promoting AE in Seattle.

In a matter of days, Ebe was in Seattle for an interview. The process was condensed into a couple of days as he met with them for the second and third interviews. There was just one free morning, when someone took the prospective head of the department of missions for a short tour. Many thoughts of Seattle came flooding into Ebe's mind, of landmarks like the Space Needle and the revolving restaurant on top of it. One funny thought was that of a competition that took place just outside the Space Needle. A number of men were competing to see who could eat the most donuts within a given number of minutes! He had never seen anything like it! They hardly chewed their donuts, but simply crushed and pushed them down with their fingers. It was more than just funny to Ebe, but also somewhat revolting!

A nobler thought was that of the Jepson family, which accommodated missionaries and evangelists in their "Prophet's Chamber." Mr. Jepson had long since passed away, leaving his wonderful wife and three daughters. That lovely family was given to catering to God's servants. Their house was on the Pacific Ocean. Ebe remembered enjoying breakfast with them on the deck, feeling as though he was sailing on a boat with water coming in and disappearing under the deck. They were joking about the possibility of someone getting sea sickness! They told stories of how Mr. Jepson had cofounded a mission called the Christian Nationals Evangelism Commission (CNEC). They shared how Dr. Billy Graham had used their prophet's chamber in his earlier days of ministry. What an honour it was to be where Billy Graham once was!

After the completion of the interviews, they offered Ebe the position. He was asked to return to Canada, discuss it with his wife and family, and see if that was what the Lord wanted him to do at that point. He was shown his office, his secretary, and the young man who would be his assistant. He would have a million-dollar budget to manage and work with. He would also be responsible to raise funds. This was all overwhelming and scary. Ebe had never handled that kind of responsibility. In North America, people talked about a million dollars as though it were a thousand dollars. The budget became one of the main reasons to turn down this amazing offer. The other reason, though to a lesser extent, was the fact that he was still working on his doctorate at Trinity Evangelical Divinity

School (TEDS), even though it was pretty close to completion. Ebe and his wife Emily felt that they were just settling down in Canada with their children. Uprooting again would be too much, in spite of all the advantages that came with the new position, even with all the contacts they had in Washington State. In fact, their three sons went to the Seattle area straight from South Africa. In retrospect, one would have to get into the boots of a black person who grew up under apartheid South Africa to appreciate how scary such "a quick rise to responsibility" would be.

XIV
SOME OBC HIGHLIGHTS

We have heard and used the expression, "God has a sense of humour." It was ironic that God would take someone from Africa—South Africa, of all places—and lead him to Canada to train Canadian nationals to be missionaries. Some missions in South Africa would not even let its own nationals teach missionaries isiZulu. They would rather depend on and trust veteran missionaries to do it. Listening to a missionary struggling in isiZulu, you could tell without hesitation who had taught them. They would repeat mistakes inherited from their teachers, who had translated some phrases literally from English to isiZulu. Once people learn a wrong thing, it's very difficult to unlearn it. It was appropriate to learn from the "originals," be it culture, custom, or language. Students found it very profitable to interact with, and have their questions answered by, someone who had not learned from some foreigner.

SOME OBC HIGHLIGHTS

Annual Missions Conference

Missions played a very important part of the college. A Missions Conference was held for one week each year. Classes were suspended and the entire student body was required to attend. Missionaries came from many missions in North America and brought with them their displays. They came to share their experiences with prospective missionaries and to "recruit" workers. (We ended up asking missionaries *not* to use that term, because it became unpopular among students).

There were some well-known names who came to speak at each conference (such as Ravi Zacharias, Ralph Winter, Ron Blue, Sam Kamaleson, Leighton Ford, Lori Lutz, and Roy Comrie). The same thing went for chapel. Ebenezer was Chapel Coordinator as well. He invited many well-known speakers, like Charles Price, who was still teaching at Capernwray, England. Ken Needham came from Capernwray as well. Sunder Krishnan, Keith Price, and many local pastors were invited to speak in the chapel. A lot more speakers visited his missions classes on any given year—like Eric Wright, John Miller, Hudson Taylor III, Koos Fitjie, Bob Morris, and Dick Winchell. The list could go on and on. Students were exposed to many gifted servants of the Lord, and that was the purpose. A paragraph could be written on each of the above tremendous communicators and some very significant things they shared with the student body. They covered a wide spectrum of experiences.

WRESTLING WITH APARTHEID

Field Education

Among the adjunct professors, the one who served the longest time was Miss Della Watson of Serving in Mission (SIM), formally the Sudan Interior Mission. Now it was called SIM International. She was in charge of Field Education for all Intercultural Studies majors. She was a volunteer, and an accomplished French teacher and high school teacher in Nigeria. She spent long hours working with each student scrutinizing their reports, interviewing them, and faithfully making reports and grading each student. She got to know students well and adequately met their individual needs.

This was during the time when urbanization was not only a buzz word but a huge undertaking. People were flocking to cities from rural areas looking for work. Some secular magazines were full of articles on urbanization. Projections of city populations and statistics in developing countries were mind-boggling. And, of course, Toronto was declared the world's most cosmopolitan city by the United Nations. It still is. Students had great opportunities to minister to churches, groups, and organizations in a city that was on such a cutting edge. Della was in the thick of it all. Dr. Timothy Warner, who was Ebenezer's mentor at Trinity Evangelical Divinity School, did not hesitate to encourage him to write his doctoral thesis, which he called the "Field Education Manual for Ontario Bible College Missions Majors, Toronto." This college had the distinction of being the first Bible College in Canada. It was on September 12, 1894 when the first class of the Toronto Bible College, as it was then called, was held at Walmer Road Baptist Church. The history provided a rich field of research, and a very rewarding one at that.

Students' Missions Committee

Ebe, who proposed a name change from Missions Department to Intercultural Studies, worked with a Missions Committee consisting of students to plan each conference. His title was changed to "Coordinator of Intercultural Studies." These changes came about as a result of a group of "Professors of Missions," which convened at Fuller Theological Seminary, School of World Missions California. It was found inadvisable to issue diplomas stating that a student had graduated as a "Missions Major." The word *Missions* should not be on the diploma, because it revealed that the person holding it was there to proselytize. They needed to be creative in entering such countries. That was one of the things that triggered all the changes.

The coordinator of Intercultural Studies was very impressed with the giftedness and commitment displayed by students who served on the committee. Ebe noticed this from the very first committee he worked with, elected in 1980. Students took initiatives. They were capable and creative. They came up with the theme of each conference. They decided on the logo. Subcommittees (such as Publicity, Program, and Finance) diligently worked on their assignments and brought good reports to the next meeting. Leadership skills began to emerge and to be obvious. It came as no surprise to see and hear of some of those who later became very distinguished missionaries and Christian leaders in the ministry.

Even now, Ebe hardly enters a Christian gathering without someone recognizing him and coming up to introduce themselves to him as being a former student of his.

A Setback

One setback Ebe experienced with one year left before his retirement was a situation well-known in Canada, which was beyond the control of the college. The college and seminary came close to declaring bankruptcy! The Lord rescued it when the school was teetering on the brink. Now, it is fully recovered under the leadership of Dr. Brian Stiller. In fact, later, the administration purchased a chunk of almost adjoining property to accommodate their growth. But during the crisis, a number of professors had to be let go.

Ebe left at the same time, but had already been granted his sabbatical with pay. The laid-off faculty had to go to the unemployment office, apply for unemployment, and look for new jobs. He stood no chance of getting such a job. He went to World Vision for an interview, but was not taken. As he sat there awaiting his turn to be interviewed, one of his students came and sat in line for the same job! Another friend had advised him to apply for a position to deliver pizza at night. Mr. Sub on Yonge Street took him on to deliver subs! He was there for probably two or three days. He left it, the reasons being that it was dangerous to do that at night and he also saw a scenario where he might knock on an apartment door and be met by a former student.

So he left and volunteered at the North York Hospital on Leslie Street. Eventually, he gave up looking for a job and decided to stick with the little church north of Stouffville, which he was already helping part-time. He was concerned about his and Emily's retirement, because there was no retirement benefits coming from either the college or Emily's school. Neither of them qualified for a full Canada pension, as they had not worked long enough in Canada. Emily's retirement was fast approaching, too.

Rejoining African Enterprise

Michael Cassidy was invited to speak at a Promise Keepers convention in Charlotte, North Carolina. Malcolm, executive director of African Enterprise in California, invited him to join them in manning the AE booth. From Charlotte, they were to go on to the next Promise Keepers convention in Chicago. They formed a good team representing AE at those two conventions.

Michael and Malcolm invited Ebe to have breakfast with them in his hotel in Chicago. There, they discussed the possibility of rejoining AE and helping to promote AE in the United States and Canada. African Enterprise then offered him another part-time ministry. He tried to raise support both in the United States and in Canada, but the response was not overwhelming. But there were some faithful supporters for whom they were very deeply thankful. Their daughter, and her husband Jim, committed to supporting them for many years.

Churchill Community Church

Ebe also served as pastor of a small church which had a history of splits, but the church didn't experience another split in the twelve years he was there. He was part-time. The small congregation could not provide the pastor with a secretary, or other conveniences enjoyed by pastors in bigger churches. The attendance increased sometimes, but then decreased again when younger families moved on. At some point, they even had three physicians in their church. Ebe worked on the history of the church, adding to what he found in the church files, and updating it in preparation for the 125th celebration of its existence. That was when he discovered that he was the longest serving pastor of that church.

Vacation in Arizona

Something significant happened during that time. Their daughter Primrose and her husband, Stan, bought them airline tickets to go to Arizona for a vacation! A couple from their church, Dr. and Mrs. Norman Musewe, were in a timesharing program after Dr. Musewe's wife, Endra, worked hard finding accommodation. The Sikakanes had a wonderful time in Arizona, getting around in a rented car. Arizona was chosen because it would give Emily a bit of relief from the arthritis that she had. And it was some relief, indeed. The only time they did not need a car was when they got on a tour bus to see the spectacular Grand Canyon. What a sight that was! Psalm 19 took on a brand new meaning, as they discussed it there and the rest of their days in Arizona. The tour guide was excellent and he knew the place well and pointed out things along the road to us. This was one of those *times of refreshing [that] come from the presence of the Lord*" (Acts 3:19, NKJV).

There were many wonderful opportunities of ministry in this small congregation apart from preaching on Sunday mornings, with Sunday evening service once a month and Bible study on Tuesdays. There were open air services in summer, Vacation Bible School (VBS), and for young people, periodical visitation to the community. There were also special occasions when meetings were taken to the community by holding them in the local community center. Opportunities were also created by outsiders coming to the church requesting the dedication of their children, or asking to be married or buried. Throughout all these avenues, people heard the Gospel.

One funeral service that stood out in Ebe's mind was that of a ninety-six-year-old lady, Carrie McLaughlin, who drove her own car until she was ninety-three. She started asking Ebe to conduct her funeral long before she died. Ebe used to joke each time she raised the subject by saying that he might die before she did. She was one of the pillars of the church, indeed, and her funeral was a victorious occasion. The appropriate message was based on 2 Timothy 4:6-8, where Paul said, *"The time of my departure has come. I have fought the good fight. I have finished the race, I have kept the faith… there is laid up for me the crown of righteousness"* (ESV).

WRESTLING WITH APARTHEID

Trip to South Africa—Oxford—Paris

One of the greatest trips that Ebe and Emily undertook before their retirement, which was financed by friends' air miles, was spending a few days in England with their former friend from South Africa, Tonia Cope. She was a teacher in Pietermaritzburg and attended Chapel Street Baptist Church. She was a great friend of African Enterprise who financially supported Ebe and Emily. She was so committed to the ministry of Bonginkosi (in isiZulu, meaning "Praise the Lord") that she continued to support and promote it. She married an engineer, Stephen Bowley. This couple took them to the campus of Oxford, where she worked for a professor. They took them around to see the many historical buildings associated with names like C.S. Lewis and John Wesley.

From Oxford, they went to South Africa to spend time with their brothers and sisters and their families. It was a very refreshing time. They spent some time visiting friends as well. It was great to see the progress that the Union Bible Institute had made. They spent a few days at the African Enterprise Centre. It was always surprising to go back to these places where they had spent a good part of their lives and find so many new faces. It made them feel like strangers.

Finally, they flew to Paris on their way home. It was their first time there. A former student of Ebe, Claudine Horalla, met them at the airport and spent nearly a week showing them around that gorgeous city. They stayed in a castle which had been converted into a Bible school by Greater Europe Mission. Even though Claudine was neither a student nor a teacher, she knew a good number of people at the school. In fact, Claudine was a nurse in a different city.

Bermuda

In the year 2000, Ebe received an unexpected invitation from a friend, Reverend Bill Lamb and his wife Gina. Bill asked him to speak for a special group of people at the Willowbank Hotel in Bermuda. This event took place every February. All Ebe knew was that he would lead Bible studies first thing after breakfast. It appealed to Ebe, and after a few days discussing it with Emily, he accepted. The subsequent details made it overwhelming to him, though. The people who attended the annual gathering came mainly from Canada and the United States. There were indeed more Canadians than Americans that year. They met there once a year just to relax and vacation at that prestigious resort. It was only then that Bill explained that the featured speaker for that year was to have been Dr. Gladstone, and that he had suddenly taken ill and could not go to Bermuda. Ebe thought that if that was the calibre of speakers those people were accustomed to, he was going to find it hard to fill those shoes. But Bill reassured and encouraged him to go. He did.

It was quite an experience for Ebe. Many of the people there seemed to be a well-to-do bunch who had retired well and were there to enjoy their time on that historic island. Nonetheless, they were very accepting and simply a wonderful group of people.

There was Dr. Bill Berg, a retired Lutheran Minister from Minneapolis, who was over ninety years of age and provided leadership to this great ministry, along with Bill from Toronto. He was a dynamic speaker for a man his age. Another black gentleman present was also named Ebenezer, a Rwandan residing in Canada with his wife Anna-Marie!

People seemed to enjoy the Book of Esther, which they studied together. At the end of their time, they extended an invitation to Ebe to return the following year. Dr. Berg promised to bring three generations of his family to listen, for the first time, to the preaching of an umZulu from South Africa. And they surely showed up the following year. Emily, who could not go to Bermuda in 2000 because of previous commitments, did attend the second time, and she enjoyed it immensely. There was ample time to go on excellent sightseeing tours, and there was lots to see.

One of the many interesting things they learned was that there was no river on the island. People depended on rain water caught from the roofs of buildings. Roofs were all painted the same colour—white—to keep water clean. The world's shortest bridge was in Bermuda. It was eighteen inches wide— yes, eighteen inches! It was opened to let small boats with tall masts pass through. The island uses American currency and has quite a high cost of living.

Trips to the White House

Ebe made two trips to the White House in Washington D.C. The first one was during the time when Mr. Schultz was Secretary of State, in the 1980s. He invited a number of South Africans living in North America to participate in a dialogue with officials of his department on the problem of apartheid. There were a handful of them from Canada who were basically intended to be a resource. They participated in small group discussions. Very few of them, if any, gave a significant paper. Most of those were given by African Americans who had made trips to South Africa. But that would naturally be different from a paper given by someone who had actually grown up under the apartheid system.

It was interesting and depressing at the same time to see and hear people like the late Dr. Jerry Falwell returning from a couple of weeks' visit to South Africa, speaking very authoritatively on the issues of apartheid. They would go there as guests of the South Africa government. The government planned their itinerary. They would line up a number of black leaders to be interviewed, who were supportive of apartheid. Such ill-informed people returned to the United States declaring that Nelson Mandela was a communist who would destroy South Africa if he ever became its leader. Now the world knows how mistaken they were. (There were no African Americans among them). Some had simply not been in South Africa long enough to fully understand apartheid.

The second time Ebe went to the White House was in 2004. He was hosted by the Senate Chaplain, Dr. Black. His capable secretary, Miss Meg Saunders, handled all the arrangements for Ebe to come to Capitol Hill. He was to stay at the Washington Retreat House, which was owned by Roman Catholics and located near the Catholic University. It was convenient to commute to Capitol Hill from the Washington Retreat. He was to meet with Chaplain Black personally. This meeting took place right after the Bible study session which he led. He was a very impressive Bible teacher. Then he had a meeting with Senator Bill Nelson's aide, who handled his foreign affairs; then, Senator Jim Inhofe's aide; and finally, Senator Frist's Chief of Staff. He finally met with Michelle DeKonty of Global Health and AIDS Division, whose boss reported directly to President Bush. The reason for the meeting was to discuss the HIV/AIDS in South AFrica. These Christian senators were interested in helping Christian organizations involved in dealing with the situation in South Africa. Ebe came armed with the latest information and statistics gathered from papers from the South African Christian Leadership Assembly, organized by African Enterprise. The problem AE encountered was that they had to raise a substantial sum of money prior to qualifying for faith-based organization benefits. But senators were really committed to assisting the poorest countries. For instance, Dr. Frist, Ebe learned, spent his own private funds flying out to do operations in the "poorest" countries.

Even though these were the only two times Ebe went to Capitol Hill on behalf of South Africa, he actually had been there once before. When Dr. Dick Halverson was Chaplain of the Senate, Ebe had gone to speak at a men's breakfast. He remembered that after speaking to the fairly large group of men, he sat at the head table next to the chairman. The chairman told him two things. He was not calling himself a *converted* Jew, but a *completed* Jew. Secondly, he said, "I did not tell you before you spoke that all the people you see here are legal people—lawyers, judges etc." Ebe would have certainly felt uncomfortable, even though he was not preaching but telling them about the ministry of African Enterprise.

African Enterprise—Part-time

Ebe continues to work part-time for AE. He goes to churches in the United States by invitation. He also initiates some trips both in Canada and the United States. The invitations that Ebe initiates come about as a result of visits to North America by team leaders and team members from Africa to promote AE. He coordinates dates and times of such visits with churches, missions committees, and groups who are interested in the ministry of AE. He always bears in mind that possible new supporters are included in these groups. Flight reservations are coordinated—from east to west and vice versa. Arrangements for the accommodation and ground transportation of visitors are important factors. In some cases, Ebe accompanies them from, say, New York to New Jersey to Oklahoma to Colorado and across the border to Canada and back to Africa. Ebe's main responsibility is to set up the AE's promotional display. He does some speaking to adult Sunday school classes and youth groups. He sometimes travels alone to churches, attending Missions conferences as a speaker or just to talk about AE ministry in Africa.

It has been a great learning experience seeing all the creative ways in which different churches raise funds to support missionaries. One church in Canada does this via Faith Promise. They raise about two million dollars a year for missions only. They fly in a couple of missionaries from every continent that they support. Another church in the United States raises thousands of dollars "on the spot" during the missions conference. The attendance in this particular church is amazing. The senior pastor and the missions committee receive special projects for which the invited representatives will request support. Prior to the conference, these are submitted for the church to pray for. When the four days of the missions conference come, the senior pastor prayerfully announces the amount needed for each project and asks for individuals to give amounts ranging from a thousand dollars down and they respond by a show of hands. He and the missions pastor keep track of amounts. This happens each evening and it takes about twenty minutes to raise funds for about ten missionaries. Cheques are made out to the church. The mission project is specified on the cheque. This happens and works every time.

XV
SOME SPECIAL
MEMORIES

Mbabane, Capital of Swaziland

Ebe was invited by the Africa Evangelical Fellowship (AEF) to speak at a pastors' conference. Pastors came from every part of Swaziland. Among them were some who had graduated from the Union Bible Institute whom he knew as his former students. Such occasions were like refresher courses for the UBI graduates.

In that region of Mbabane, there was a good Child Evangelism Fellowship ministry. It was organized by a Miss Carmichael both in Swaziland and South Africa. It was thriving under the leadership of a Swazi lady, Anna Dlamini. She was a good friend of Betty and Mel Swanson. In fact, she was "adopted" by the Swansons the same way they had "adopted" Emily and Ebe. Anna was a very devoted follower of the Lord and a very mature Christian. She was working very diligently to win children to Christ. Some of the pastors did not have Child Evangelism Fellowship operating in their area. According to arrangements, Anna would bring a group of non-Christian herd-boys (young boys who tended herds of cattle), who did not attend Sunday school anywhere. They were going to be attending Anna's class and in all probability hearing the Gospel for the first time. Using her flannel board, she made a presentation of the Gospel with limpid clarity in the presence of the pastors. Nearly the whole class made what seemed like a genuine commitment to Christ, and some of the boys were in tears. When she finished praying with them, she gave them a further assurance of their forgiveness of sin and God's forgiveness. That demonstration made an incredible impact on the pastors who were there.

Manzini, Swaziland

Manzini was the second of the two largest cities in Swaziland, by their standard. Ebe had been to Manzini a number of times to preach and teach, but this time the whole family was there for a vacation. They had been invited by the head of the large Nazarene hospital, Dr. Hind. They did not often get these vacations, but AE encouraged them to go. They all had lots of fun just driving to Swaziland. The five children had never been to Swaziland, so they were very excited. They arrived at the hospital in the early afternoon.

Mrs. Hind, the doctor's wife, welcomed them warmly, accompanied by her sister-in-law who had also just arrived for a visit from England. After entertaining them with some light refreshments, she showed them their rooms. She then left and was going to come and fetch them later for dinner, where they would discuss plans for the few days they were there. Everything sounded super. There was no discrimination in Swaziland.

Shortly before dinner, a Swazi lady came to them and spoke standing at the door, *"Baba noma-ke Sikakane,unkosikazi sawufile."* ("Father and mother Sikakane, Mrs. Hind has died.") She paused, struggling with composure and holding back tears. To say they were shocked would be an understatement! Emily said, "Heart attack?"

"No. Car accident."

"Had she gone to town?"

"No. Right within the mission station!"

Apparently, Mrs. Hind's sister-in-law had been driving the car, and she ran over her while reversing it! That was probably one of the saddest funerals the Sikakanes had ever attended. You can't even imagine how her sister-in-law must have felt those days. Dr. Hind comforted his sister and totally forgave her, because she would never have done such a thing intentionally to her best friend.

Mosvold Mission Hospital

Ebe made a number of trips to Mosvold Mission Hospital over a period of years. He spoke to nurses at several graduation ceremonies. There was a high level of commitment to spiritual life at this hospital. Doctors, nurses, clerks, and even patients understood that the way they were loved and cared for was because of the Gospel. Auntie Sithole was a highly respected matron at Mosvold. She had a responsible position as matron, and everyone loved her and spoke highly of her faith.

Dr. Don Morrell was concerned about the distances people had to travel on foot to get to the hospital. Other means of travel were not readily available in the rural area surrounding the hospital. When they embarked on a big project of immunization, Morrell established at least one immunization posts, and maybe more. One of these became so busy that they built a fairly large hall, built of wattle and daub, several miles away from Mosvold Hospital. It was used for immunization as well as a preaching post, with a view toward planting a church. A big evangelistic thrust was planned and they invited Ebe to run a series of meetings in that hall. A good number of people and missionaries were in attendance each evening. The results were good also.

One afternoon, after preaching on John 8 ("The truth will set you free"), and after pinpointing specific things and lies that enslave people's souls, and things from which only Jesus, who is "the Truth" can set them free, a group of people stayed behind so they could pray with them as they committed their lives to Christ. This time, something unusual happened. There was a lady who behaved strangely, and trembling like a reed she announced that she had been sent to Durban to be trained as a witch doctor. She was consequently filled with the evil spirits. She wanted to be set free from them. Ebe had never been confronted by such a situation before, though he had heard many such stories. Nonetheless, he assured her that Christ was going to set her free. There were a few other Christians who had stayed behind to pray individually with those who were seeking salvation.

He asked those Christians not to be involved with the witch doctor's case if they did not feel free to do so. He did this because some of them appeared uneasy as they listened to the lady that he was about to pray for. All of them left except for Auntie Sithole. So he laid hands on the lady and commanded the evil spirits in Christ's name to get out. They did. After some time, she woke up as from a deep sleep, relieved, and her face almost shone. They spent time with her, assuring her of Christ's freedom which she had received. Finally, she asked them to accompany her to her home, which was close by. She explained that she wanted to get rid of all the stuff that she was using for witchcraft. While they were preparing to leave for her home, she asked them to delay a while, and she went ahead to prepare for their coming.

When she was ready, they started for her home. Nurse Preece was a Canadian nurse in charge of training nurses in the hospital. She had been there with one or two other nurses, all the time just praying through the whole process which they could not follow in detail as they did not speak isiZulu well. By now, they were fully briefed. Miss Preece drove them in her blue Volkswagen to the lady's home. To their utter amazement, she had done two things. Firstly, she had sent for her neighbours to come and witness what she was about to do with all the witchcraft stuff that she had. Secondly, she had cleared her medicine hut of all the paraphernalia that she used in her profession. She piled it all up to about the size of her hut. There were dry leaves, roots, goat skins, cow hides, bones, and gall bladders (pumped up like balloons). She explained carefully to her neighbours that she had become a Christian and was no longer going to be dabbling in witchcraft again. She then introduced Ebe and explained that she had asked him to come and burn all her evil stuff. Her neighbours watched askance, dumb-founded and in disbelief, as the "sacred" paraphernalia went up in smoke.

The incident that happened in Ephesus while Paul was there came to Ebe's mind, and so he read from the Bible, "*Also many of those who were now believers came, confessing and divulging their practices. And a number of those who had practiced magic arts brought their books together and burned them in the sight of all. And they counted the value of them and found it came to fifty thousand pieces of silver. So the Word of the Lord continued to increase and prevail mightily*" (Acts 19:18-20, ESV). After proclaiming the power of the Gospel, he set the paraphernalia alight. The Mosvold pastor and women folk committed to nurturing and discipling the new convert. After a couple of years, Ebe met with someone from Mosvold and he asked about the witch doctor. They told him that she had grown spiritually so much that she had become a "Bible woman" (a sort of itinerant Bible teacher who visited, read the Bible, and prayed with women).

Greenville Mission Hospital

Greenville was a Free Methodist Mission Hospital in the Transkei with dedicated missionaries. They were dedicated to the Lord and also to working themselves out of a job by consistently training black staff for positions of leadership, even in their mission stations. At Greenville, there were interesting dynamics. There was the "old stock" South African born missionaries who were committed to running and managing black churches for as long as they lived. When they were out of the scene, their kids would take over. But then, the younger American missionaries, Elmore Clyde and Warren Johnson, were different. There was bound to be a generational chasm that needed to be gulfed. Discussions at dinner tables were interesting—more than just interesting, when senior South African guys did not feel free to sit at the table with a black man, Ebe, but the younger missionaries wanted to do so. That was the extent to which discrimination and racism had gone in South Africa.

Otherwise, the ministry in Greenville was tremendous. Black nurses, nurses in training, the administrative staff, blue collar employees, patients, and outpatients were all very receptive to the Gospel. There was obvious spiritual hunger in some, and growth in others. This could be said with all the mission hospitals Ebe spoke at in South Africa. There were, however, obviously those who were indifferent. The counselling sessions which consumed Ebe's time and as a speaker were the most encouraging, as he could evaluate the extent to which those who responded to his message were affected by it. Ebe learned a lot from Elmore Clyde and Warren Johnson during their times of prayer together with the young men they were mentoring. The missionaries and their wives really believed in the power of prayer and intercession.

WRESTLING WITH APARTHEID

Bethesda Mission Hospital

The Bethesda Mission Hospital was in Zululand (now KwaZulu-Natal). Overall, there seemed to be a smaller percentage of young people and young adults who understood the Gospel. Yet, there was a great openness to it. As people heard it, they were willing to commit their lives to Christ. Ebe had an interesting experience at this hospital. There was only one white man who attended the evening service. He spoke isiZulu very well, and so he understood the message.

When the appeal was made, he came forward to commit his life to Christ, crying like a child. Everything was running down his face, eyes, and nose. He did not have a handkerchief or a tissue. Ebe could not believe how difficult it was for him to counsel a white person. It was the first time this had ever happened to him in that kind of setting. He hurried through the whole process and prayed for him and let him go.

One incident that had just happened in this rural area of South Africa, which was recounted to Ebe, was a very sad one. A black man walked through the farm of a white man, taking a shortcut because he was rushing. People walked long distances because there were no buses. What he did not realize was that the farmer was nearby watching him. The furious farmer stopped him and questioned this man who had such audacity as to walk through his farm. Not having any excuse that would satisfy the farmer, he simply apologized again and gain. The farmer promised to teach him a lesson that he would never forget. He pulled out just about all his teeth with a pair of pliers or pincers, leaving him semi-conscious! Often a white man would never be accused of wrong or prosecuted for doing even a horrific and criminal act as this to a black person.

Edendale Government Hospital

Edendale Hospital was about twenty minutes from the Union Bible Institute. It was a show-piece built by the government to prove that apartheid was good for blacks and that it really meant parallel development. The once immaculate hospital had now degenerated to something almost disgraceful. It was bound to be, because there was never a budget to maintain it in the long-term. It was unrealistic for the apartheid government to find sufficient funds to budget for both affluent white South Africans as well as the ten additional black states that would depend on South Africa for a long time before becoming self-supporting in the poorest parts assigned to them. Therefore, the hospital started running out of simple tablets long before 1994, perhaps mainly because Chief Gatsha Buthelezi had refused the independence that the white government had offered him. So they were going to penalize him.

Be that as it may, the UBI students led by Ebe had great opportunities of ministry during its hay day. From his UBI to AE days, there were wonderful opportunities to reach what would be described as the cream of the crop in South Africa. The nurses were like a hand-picked bunch of young ladies in their immaculately white uniforms, maroon shoulder-loops, and bright red capes! There was a very strong Christian Nurses Fellowship. The UBI choir was invited there often. There would be a concert and a message with a good response.

Sometimes an invitation came from the Nurses Fellowship for a speaker. Ebe was the one usually assigned to that opportunity.

Apartheid was always acting like a spoiler. One day, Ebe got a phone call from a white lady in Edendale asking him to bring students to sing at the nurses' hall. They got there as requested, and they went straight to the familiar hall to ensure that the chairs were arranged ahead of time for the nurses and for the choir. As they were doing that, the lady who had called stormed into the hall and asked for the man she had spoken to. Ebe identified himself. He knew at once that he was in trouble. Her grim face told the whole story.

"Who are all these men?" she asked.

"This is the choir you requested, madam."

"Why did you bring so many? Couldn't you bring four of five of them? Where are my nurses going to sit now?"

He tried to explain calmly that he had no quartet. This was the only singing group at UBI. She stood with her hands on her hips and looked at him the usual way whites looked at blacks, as though to pounce on him. As it transpired, there was no seating problem at all. The meeting went without a hitch. When the students were getting on the truck to leave, some students stood around Ebe and asked, "Why did we stay? We should have just left." He tried to give them a short improvised lecture about how Christians should never fight fire with fire... flesh with flesh. As he drove home, he felt like another voice was saying, "You have been a good model to your students. They realized how spiritual you are." He immediately felt a rebuke in the spirit. The voice seemed to say, too, "The evil one failed to get you to fight the white lady. Now he is sneaking in through the back door with spiritual pride!" That was a timely Word from the Lord for Ebe, one which he never forgot.

McCord Hospital

McCord Hospital was situated in the beautiful coastal city of Durban, which was popular among respectable white and blacks along the coastal belt of Natal. The first two of the Sikakanes' children were born at McCord, even though they were not the elite by any means. Emily stayed with the family Ebe's cousin, a senior minister of the Methodist Church, Enos and Winnie Sikakane. They rushed Emily to hospital when she was ready to enter the labour ward. Ebe was away teaching in the Stanger district. The mission station had no telephone. The local Indian trading store had one, a mile away from the school. That was how Ebe got the news of the arrival of both of their kids. The hospital was built by the American Board Mission. They built churches and good schools along the coast. In the Stanger area, they had a mission station called Groutville. That was one of the missions that greatly enhanced Christianity in Natal. There were lots of educated people who owned and farmed land. The most popular leader and brilliant politician who founded the African National Congress made Groutville his home. This was Chief Albert Luthuli.

The ministry to McCord Hospital was opened up by a friend of Ebe's who worked at the hospital, Esau Nxele. He was a member of the great Umgeni Road Baptist Church. The gifted minister William Duma was the senior pastor of Umgeni Road. Esau was an employee of McCord Hospital. He had an outstanding testimony in the hospital. Pastor Duma had affected this hospital positively with the Gospel. There were opportunities to minister to the hospital workers, who were non-professionals but equally strategic. There were opportunities there to strengthen the Christians in their faith and growth as well as to make first-time commitments.

Esau left McCord to start his business from scratch. It seemed as if everything he touched turned to gold. He has become a prosperous Christian businessman who never studied anything about business. His several trading stores became centres of evangelism. Esau invited Ebe to hold evangelistic meetings for his employees and neighbours a number of times. These were successful outreaches. He saw his businesses as a means of reaching people with the Gospel in rural KwaZulu Natal. He spent one week at a time living in the home of the Sikakanes, attending lectures at Union Bible Institute. He and his wife, Lillian, have now planted a number of Baptist churches around areas where he had stores and butcher shops. He is a gifted preacher. It all began at McCord Hospital!

Murchison Mission Hospital

This Brethren Hospital was situated on the border of KwaZulu Natal and Transkei. Some very devoted missionaries worked in the hospital. It was a big surprise for the Sikakanes, upon arriving in Toronto some twenty-eight years later, to find there a couple who had worked in Murchison.

SOME SPECIAL MEMORIES

Dr. Norman and Mrs. Doreen Bier have now been close friends with the Sikakanes since they re-established their relationship. The Biers very graciously provided the following very old report and photographs of the meetings of the Hospital Christian Fellowship Conference, held at Murchison Hospital where Ebe was the speaker in June 1973. The author of the report, Nurse A. Ramza, wrote:

> "It was a great pleasure to me to be chosen as one of the delegates to the Conference. Many nurses from other hospitals in Natal and the Transkei also came, arriving on Friday and staying until Sunday afternoon. Mr. Sikakane from African Enterprise was the speaker, and the theme was 'How to lead someone to Christ.'
>
> Mr. Sikakane gave five lectures from Mark's Gospel: (1) Go Into All the World (Mark 16:15ff). (2) Three Great Truths Every Christian Should Know About Mankind. (3) Jesus Christ, the Only Saviour of Mankind. (4) How the Sinner Meets the Saviour. (5) Assurance of Salvation.
>
> I gained many things from the conference, but the first day I realized that although all along I was calling myself a Christian, I was not. I was lost. Then I saw that being a Christian does not mean going to church or even preaching. The conference as a whole brought me a new life. I thought I was a Christian, but I found I was still a sinner as God said in His Word. I hope I will follow Mr Sikakane's warnings which he gave us during the farewell meeting."

WRESTLING WITH APARTHEID

Teaming With Dr. Ravi Zacharias

Ebe emphasized that when he was asked to share the pulpit with Dr. Zacharias some twenty-five years ago, it was not the man he hears now. It was during the earlier days of Dr. Zacharias, before he went to further his studies in England. Nonetheless, it was an honour to sit at his feet even then.

The Free Methodist Church invited them to minister in Spring Arbor, Michigan in 1983. It was during their National Missions Conference. It was a great privilege for Ebe to share the platform with a speaker of such great stature. They challenged the delegates with a clear message on the mission of the church. The Free Methodist is, no doubt, fully committed to missions. They have highly trained missionaries—doctors, nurses, Christian educators, etc. Ebe and Dr. Zacharias spent some time on a tour of Winona Lake. This was where the Free Methodist headquarters were situated. Their college, Grace College, was also at Winona Lake. It was a beautiful location.

Central Africa Health Care Organization

Another wonderful time Ebe had with the Free Methodist Church was in the year 2002. This was a large organization of medical personnel who were missionaries in Africa, though some were retired. Others are still working, mainly in Central Africa, and still others, doctors in training, will be working in Africa. It was their twelfth annual Spring Conference. Ebe was one of five speakers. They were all wonderful Free Methodist medical personnel except Ebe. They included doctors and nurses with testimonies and visions of young people burning to get to the mission field, but were already involved in the ministry. It was a great gathering with lots of collective experiences to learn from. The spirit of servanthood simply permeated everything, and that provided a very special richness and blessing to the conference.

XVI
POST-RETIREMENT

The Peoples Church

W hen Ebe finally stepped down from Churchill Community Church, not yet sure as to what to do next, something extraordinary happened. On the Monday preceding his last Sunday at the church, Dr. Timothy Starr of Peoples Church called early in the morning and, out of the blue, asked if it was true that he was leaving Churchill. He confirmed that he was. Then Starr said, "Can we meet for lunch at noon today?" He agreed. So they met. Starr offered him an opportunity to help him in his ministry, then called "North of Forty." Six days later, when Ebe preached his final message, he announced his new appointment! People responded in disbelief.

Soon after starting on this Peoples Church ministry, Reg Andrews, Executive Pastor, asked Emily and Ebe to have lunch with him. He asked Ebe to help in the leadership of the Alpha Course. This was a great opportunity to be a part of this great church. Their acquaintance with the senior pastor, Dr. Charles Price, went back to 1973 when he had attended the Congress on Mission and Evangelism in Durban, South Africa. He had always been a great blessing. They had further connected in Canada when Ebe, who was Chapel Coordinator at Tyndale, invited Pastor Price to speak at the college. He was coming from Capernwray that time.

Other opportunities given to Ebe at Peoples were to co-teach and organize the Alpha Course, teach an elective course, do some Bible study at the prayer meetings, as well as assist Dr. Starr in the seniors' luncheon on Saturdays once a month. Finally, they accepted Ebe and Emily as missionaries representing AE at the World Missions Conference.

Ministry to Seniors

Shortly after the Sikakanes became members of the church, Dr. Timothy Starr noticed that Richview Baptist Church in Etobicoke needed a Pastor to Seniors. He encouraged Ebe to apply for that part-time position. So, Emily and Ebe were thankful to the Lord for that opportunity. They had to learn all they could about the seniors' ministry from Starr. Ebe was greatly assisted by Dr. Darryl Dash, senior pastor of Richview Baptist Church, and by Miss Arlene Rawson, Director of the Richview Residence. The Sikakanes are at present living in their own apartment at Richview Residence. They started out small, calling the ministry to seniors "Joy Fellowship (Just Older Youth)." They gradually introduced services for seniors, starting with a Bible study held every Tuesday morning, a luncheon held once every two months, and a Hymn Sing, held one Sunday evening per month. There are several other areas of ministry they are involved in.

CONCLUSION

E be concluded his story by expressing his marvel at the grace and mercy of God. He was reminded of the prayer that Jacob prayed while returning from Laban's home as he prepared to meet his brother Esau. He and Emily could truly identify with Jacob, who said, *"I am not worthy of the least of all the deeds of steadfast love and all the faithfulness that you have shown to your servant, for with only my staff I crossed this Jordan, and now I have become two camps"* (Genesis 32:10, ESV). And we can sing Emily's favourite hymn, *Great is Thy Faithfulness:* "Morning by morning new mercies I see. All I have needed Thy hand hath provided; Great is Thy faithfulness, Lord, unto me!" (based on Lamentations 3:23)

They were young when they first met at ETTC. After getting married at Ekuthandaneni Mission Station, they started their family. The first two children were very young when they moved to the Union Bible Institute. Three of them were born in Edendale Hospital, near Pietermaritzburg. Ebe and Emily sought to nurture them in the knowledge of the Lord. The family altar, which was hardly ever missed, was every evening after supper. They read and discussed Bible stories using a big kids' book of Bible stories from Genesis. The kids loved the big coloured pictures. They gave their lives to Christ either there or at their Sunday School, taught by UBI students. They were all baptized at the Baptist Church in Sobantu Village, just outside Pietermaritzburg, when they understood what baptism was all about. Their family was more involved with the Swedish Church that was on the premises of the UBI than with the church in Sobantu, because they were ministering with UBI students every Sunday.

As they children grew up and met non-Christian kids, they continued their commitment to the church. Some kids would tease them, calling them "church boys," but it did not seem to affect them. The whole atmosphere at the Bible school was very good for them. They were sheltered from lots of bad influence. Even when they lived one year in Johannesburg for Mission '70, they enjoyed oneness in the family. They faced some situations there that made them uncomfortable. They had just arrived in Johannesburg when, as Ebe drove home from church, they saw a man beating a woman on the street. Soweto kids were laughing, jeering, and amused. All their kids were bewildered and shaken by this spectacle. What else could they expect? By God's grace, they continued to experience His faithfulness, protection, provision, and great blessing throughout Mission '70. Like Jacob crossing the Jordan, they crossed

CONCLUSION

the Atlantic Ocean with only five kids. After entering Canada, spouses were added. Soon multiplication brought nine grand-children. The most exciting of these weddings was the "double wedding," when the twins decided to wed on the same day.

Apartheid did not crush them. They and their faith went through the struggle and came out intact. This is all because the Lord says, "*When you pass through the waters, I will be with you… when you walk through the fire you shall not be burned, and the flame shall not consume you*" (Isaiah 43:2, ESV).